GREAT BRITISH STATELY HOMES

GREAT BRITISH STATELY HOMES

A PICTORIAL HISTORY

FELICITY FORSTER

SIRIUS

SIRIUS

This edition published in 2021 by Sirius Publishing, a division of
Arcturus Publishing Limited,
26/27 Bickels Yard, 151–153 Bermondsey Street,
London SE1 3HA

ISBN: 978-1-83940-709-3
AD008208UK

Printed in China

Contents

Introduction

British stately homes evoke iconic images from both history and fiction: Queen Victoria waving to her subjects from the balcony of Buckingham Palace, Winston Churchill at his desk or painting in the gardens at Chartwell, Lord and Lady Grantham entertaining royalty at Downton Abbey (Highclere Castle), or James Bond escaping from SPECTRE at Blenheim Palace.

Broadly defined as a very large and impressive historic house belonging to an aristocratic family, especially one that the public can pay to visit, a stately home may be a bespoke grand house or palace, or a converted abbey or other church building.

Terms often vary in accordance with the building's origin or importance, so a stately home might be called an abbey, castle, court, hall, house, manor, mansion, palace, park, place or priory. The term 'castle' is commonly used for a domestic residence that was once a military fortification; 'country house' is sometimes used interchangeably with 'stately home', although the latter is usually larger and grander; a 'palace' is a home belonging to royalty or a high-ranking dignitary; and in Northern Ireland the term 'big house' is used in place of 'castle', reflecting both size and importance.

KEY ELEMENTS

All stately homes share a number of qualities that set them apart from ordinary houses.

Owned by the wealthiest and most powerful people in society, stately homes are always built to inspire admiration, command respect and display power – and perhaps even to intimidate. Members of the aristocracy certainly needed them as homes

A number of stately homes, such as Newstead Abbey, had their roots in ecclesiastical buildings that were later converted into grand houses.

to live in, but they also needed them to impress, particularly when entertaining royalty, heads of state and other similarly high-ranking guests.

When it comes to scale, the general rule is 'the bigger, the better'. First impressions matter, so stately homes are normally entered via a set of large gates opening onto a long driveway flanked by symmetrical rows of trees on either side. The grounds typically consist of hundreds (or even thousands) of acres of landscaped parklands, with centuries-old trees and breathtaking panoramic views.

After a long approach that allows plenty of time for awe and admiration, there is often a centrepiece such as a lake or fountain, then a large portico above the front door. The entrance hall is the first room seen by visitors and is often the largest and most impressive room in the house, with an expansive floor space, enormous doorways and high ceilings. There

Many great houses are renowned for their beautiful settings and landscaping as here at Chatsworth in Derbyshire, which is set amidst the Peak District.

have always been heated debates as to whose stately home is the biggest or has the most rooms (for the record, Wentworth Woodhouse boasts the longest façade and greatest number of rooms).

Stately homes are frequently described with superlatives such as flamboyant, magnificent, exquisite, opulent, lavish, elegant, grand, impressive, majestic and exceptional. To this end, tremendous amounts of money are often spent on architectural design and interior decoration.

Porticos, façades, wings and domes are often made from the finest stone or brick, and windows are designed with perfect classical proportions. Bold architectural embellishments such as archways, staircases, gables, colonnades, turrets and clock towers may complete the picture.

Inside, the walls often feature rich wood panelling (wainscoting) with elaborate carvings, the ceilings may be decorated with intricate plasterwork or gilding, and the floors and staircases are made from solid wood, stone or polished marble, often adorned with fine carpets and rugs. Every surface is beautiful, and lighting is achieved by crystal or brass chandeliers, hanging pendants or stained-glass windows.

The rooms often contain stunning art collections, especially paintings by Old Masters such as Titian, Brueghel, Rubens, van Dyck, Velázquez, Rembrandt, Vermeer, Canaletto, Reynolds, Gainsborough, Goya and Turner. A formal portrait depicting the owner of the house or a family ancestor may provide the focal point above a grand fireplace. Sculptures are also important, and may be historical or contemporary.

Most stately homes are filled with valuable antiques and collectibles, including musical instruments, historical tapestries, fine furniture, books, porcelain and silver, often passed down through many generations.

The grounds are impressive, too, with manicured lawns, clipped yew hedges, herbaceous borders, fountains, ponds and trees. There is often a walled garden near the house, planted with flowers, fruit and vegetables for the kitchen, with one or more formal gardens or symmetrically patterned parterres beyond. The wider landscape may feature mazes, follies, temples, statues, lakes, woodland trails and deer parks, all with wide-ranging vistas of the surrounding countryside.

Of course, all of the above required hundreds of workers to keep everything going, so many stately homes and surrounding grounds became entire communities in their own right, necessitating additional structures such as chapels and staff cottages.

HISTORY OF STATELY HOMES

The golden era of the British stately home lasted from the 17th century until the end of the 19th century, but its history goes much further back.

Many stately homes began life as medieval monasteries or castles. Ecclesiastical buildings often had a main gate, high walls, a central open space, church, refectory, library and kitchen garden, and castles had a similarly tall outer wall with a gatehouse entrance, inner courtyard and keep (tower). Both types were often built in strategic locations such as a mountain top, hillside passage or on the bend of a river, and both demonstrated wealth and power, as well as being places of safe retreat.

The Tudor period was marked by Henry VIII's Dissolution of the Monasteries in the mid-1530s, culminating in the English Reformation, when the Church of England broke away from the Roman Catholic Church. Monasteries, abbeys, convents, priories and friaries throughout England, Wales and Ireland were disbanded and appropriated by the Crown, and then sold off to the king's favourites. Many were converted into private country homes, some revealing their true origins in the inclusion of a priest hole – a secret place in a wall or under the floorboards where

persecuted Catholics could be successfully concealed.

At the same time, the need for castles diminished after the medieval wars ended, and many fortified buildings were turned over to wealthy landowners.

Castle Howard, a magnificent house in North Yorkshire, has been home to the Howard family for more than 300 years.

Some fell into ruin, but others were preserved and transformed into grand residences designed to impress. Even in cases where a castle was replaced completely, parts of the keep or gatehouse are sometimes still visible in stately homes today.

The notion of a country house took hold in the early 17th century during the reign of James I, the era and style becoming known as 'Jacobean' (Jacobus being the Latin version of 'James'). Members of the royal court began employing architects either to design brand new buildings or to transform existing structures into larger, grander houses. The best of these were known as 'prodigy houses', designed with the specific intention of attracting and accommodating a monarch and their entourage.

By the mid-17th century, the Palladian style of architecture had become enormously fashionable throughout Britain. Inspired by the 16th-century Venetian architect Andrea Palladio, it was characterized by an adherence to classical rules of proportion and symmetry. The English architect Inigo Jones was one of its most famous exponents, his designs often featuring a temple-style portico at the front and a dome in the middle. By this time, large country houses had evolved into imposing stately homes fit for royalty.

Palladianism remained the dominant style of architecture for stately homes for the next 100 years, merging in the mid-18th century with the wider movement of neoclassicism. Neoclassical buildings could display a combination of historical styles, including ancient Greek, Roman, classical or Palladian. All were grand and dramatic, often with a vast rectangular floorplan, a flat roof with a balustrade along the edge, and a series of repeating arches or columns. The Scottish architect Robert Adam was a champion of the neoclassical style.

Gardening also underwent a revolution in the mid-18th century with the arrival of England's greatest gardener, Lancelot 'Capability' Brown. Brown designed more than 170 landscapes for British stately homes using naturalistic combinations of grass, lakes and trees that harmoniously complemented their existing surroundings.

The competition for ever-bigger, ever-grander homes continued into the 19th century, and many houses ended up a mixture of the work of two or more architects. Flamboyant and nostalgic styles were revisited, resulting in Gothic Revival, Renaissance Revival and Scottish Baronial, giving buildings gravitas as well as an air of romance.

The interiors were divided into 'above stairs' and 'below stairs'. The family lived upstairs in the State Rooms – the entrance hall, drawing rooms, dining room, ballroom, great hall, long gallery, library, music room, bedrooms and sitting rooms. The household staff occupied the downstairs areas, which typically included a steward's room, servants' corridors, vegetable scullery, pastry room, kitchen, dry larder, ice house, servants' hall, still room (distillery) and servants' quarters.

Entertainment was paramount at 18th- and 19th-century stately homes, with owners frequently hosting lavish house parties, banquet dinners, concerts, theatre performances and dances for the maximum number of guests possible. Several hundred staff lived on the premises, and were well looked after in return for their long hours of service.

As wages and taxation levels rose along with the rise in industry at the end of the 19th century, many aristocratic families found it increasingly difficult to maintain their expensive estates. Some borrowed money and others tried marrying wealthy heiresses, but World War I changed everything. Many household staff went away to war, never to return, and others sought new careers away from the service industry after the war. Bit by bit, stately homes began to decline. To keep afloat, some landowners auctioned off their heirlooms and treasures (not only paintings and artefacts, but even their interior wood panelling, flooring and fireplaces) and some homes were repurposed as convalescent hospitals for wounded soldiers. Sadly, some houses were even demolished.

Many houses, however, were preserved and restored to their former glory, either being given to the National Trust, English Heritage or an independent charity such as Historic Royal Palaces or the Royal Collection Trust, or remaining in the hands of private owners. Many homes are still inhabited today by the descendants of the original owners, with certain rooms open to the public. Some have been converted into hotels or schools, while others are scrupulously restored Grade I or II listed buildings that draw millions of visitors every year. They experience them as museums, wedding venues and wonderful places to see spectacular architecture, fine art, antique

Polesden Lacey, near Dorking in Surrey was the home of a society hostess in the early years of the 20th century.

furniture and magnficently laid-out gardens, and to learn about history.

Many stately homes have also been preserved through novels, plays, television and film. A popular genre of English detective fiction sprang up in the 1920s and 30s, in which a murder takes place in a country house (often during a snowstorm). On screen, millions of viewers revel in the activities of the fictional Robert Crawley (Earl of Grantham), Mr Darcy, Harry Potter and James Bond, as well as historical figures such as Elizabeth I, Queen Victoria, J.M.W. Turner, Winston Churchill and the Windsors.

Whether enjoyed as the setting for a book or viewed in educational documentaries or fictional dramas, stately homes provide us with amazing windows into the past, bringing the cultural and architectural history of Britain to life.

CHAPTER 1

ENGLAND
South East

England's south eastern corner has a wealth of great houses. London has many of them and is home to the monarchy at Buckingham Palace, Kensington Palace, Clarence House and Kew Palace, much loved by George III and his family. Other grand houses 'in town' include those the powerful built to mark their success such as the Duke of Wellington's Apsley House. Venture a little further out to revel in the splendour of Blenheim Palace, home to the Churchills in a 'Capability' Brown-designed landscape and Winston Churchill's home as wartime leader, Chartwell. Other architectural gems are Hampton Court Palace, built by Cardinal Wolsey and commandeered by Henry VIII, the exquisite Petworth House in Sussex, Kenwood House in Hampstead, Knole in Kent, Highclere Castle, the setting for Downton Abbey, and Stonor Park in Oxfordshire.

Kew Palace, home to George III and his family, lies in the grounds of Kew Gardens.

Apsley House

Formerly known as 'Number 1 London', Apsley House is located at Hyde Park Corner. It was once the London home of Arthur Wellesley, the Duke of Wellington, and it contains an outstanding assortment of art by Titian, Brueghel, Rubens, Velázquez, and Goya, as well as wonderful collections of silver and porcelain.

The interiors have changed little since Wellington's victory at Waterloo in 1815.

Wellington was not only a brilliant military leader but also

Today, Apsley House is under the care of English Heritage, although members of the Wellesley family still live there.

an important politician, eventually becoming Prime Minister in 1828. He needed a London residence that was appropriate for his status and suitable for entertaining. The house he chose had been designed and built for Baron Apsley by the architect Robert Adam in the 1770s – a red-brick building on the north side of Piccadilly. Wellington had the house enlarged to include a three-storey extension, a State Dining Room and new bedrooms.

After becoming Prime Minister, he made further alterations, commissioning a new staircase and the Waterloo Gallery – which was used for annual banquets to commemorate his famous victory over Napoleon. Outside, the red bricks were clad in Bath stone and a pedimented portico was added. In 1830, Wellington had to install iron bars on the ground floor windows to prevent damage during riots; this led to his famous nickname, the 'Iron Duke'.

In 1838, Wellington made provision for the contents of his house to be treated as heirlooms,

The Waterloo Gallery was designed by Benjamin Dean Wyatt to house the Duke of Wellington's collection of paintings.

forbidding any future heir to dispose of them. Wellington's son Arthur Wellesley, the 2nd Duke of Wellington, inherited the house in 1852 and decided to open it to the public. He created a Museum Room to display his father's many silver trophies, military memorabilia and gifts of porcelain.

Kenwood House

Sited on the northern boundary of Hampstead Heath in London, Kenwood House is a Georgian and neoclassical villa. It contains a fine collection of Old Master and British paintings, with works by Rembrandt, Vermeer, Gainsborough and Reynolds.

The original house was built in the early 17th century, but this was demolished and rebuilt in 1694 by the Surveyor-General of the Ordnance, William Bridges. Throughout the 18th and 19th centuries, Kenwood was the home of the Earls of Mansfield. The 1st Earl, William Murray, acquired it for £4,000 and commissioned the Scottish neoclassical architect Robert Adam to remodel the house. A library was added to complement the orangery, and small fishponds were merged to create Wood Pond and the Thousand Pound Pond.

William Murray's nephew David Murray succeeded as the 2nd Earl of Mansfield in 1793, and he added two new wings, a dining room, a music room, new kitchen buildings, a brewery and a dairy. He also hired the famous landscape gardener Humphry Repton to redesign the grounds to show them off to their best advantage, planting groves of trees, a crescent-shaped lawn and a flower garden.

Successive earls continued renovations throughout the 19th century. In 1925 it was purchased by Anglo-Irish philanthropist Edward Cecil Guinness, the 1st Earl of Iveagh. He bequeathed Kenwood House and its land to the public, to remain free of charge and be preserved as 'a fine example of the artistic home of a gentleman of the 18th century'.

The house was taken over by English Heritage in 1986. Extensive conservation work took place in 2012, and the exteriors and interiors were repainted using Robert Adam's colour scheme.

Kenwood House has been used as an elegant backdrop for many film sets, including 101 Dalmations *(1996),* Mansfield Park *(1999),* Notting Hill *(1999) and* Venus *(2006).*

Buckingham Palace

A focal point for the British public at times of royal weddings, military commemorations and national celebrations, Buckingham Palace is the London residence of the reigning monarch of the United Kingdom. As well as being a home, it has also been the administrative headquarters of the sovereign since 1837. Official functions, receptions and garden parties are held at the palace throughout the year, and the State Rooms are open to the public during the summer months.

The first house on the site – located in the City of Westminster – was constructed for the Duke of Buckingham and Normanby in 1703, designed by William Winde. It was a large three-storey block with two service wings on

either side, and was eventually bought by King George III for £21,000 in 1761. The idea was to provide his wife Charlotte with a comfortable private family home as an alternative to St James's Palace. Charlotte loved Buckingham House – 14 out of 15 of her children were born there – and it became known as 'The Queen's House'.

Upon his accession to the throne in 1820, George IV hired the services of the architect John Nash to begin remodelling the house. The main block was kept the same, but Nash doubled the size of the building by adding three wings around a central courtyard, with a triumphal arch – the Marble Arch – as a centrepiece to commemorate the battle victories at Trafalgar and Waterloo. The external walls were faced with Bath stone, reflecting the French neoclassical style.

By this time, the costs had mounted dramatically, and unfortunately George IV did not live to see the renovations completed. His younger brother, William IV, asked Edward Blore

Above: *A 19th-century representation of the Drawing Room taken from* Pyne's Royal Residences.

Left: *Changing the guard takes place on alternate days except in June and July when it happens daily.*

to finish the work, and for a time the palace was considered as a potential replacement for the Palace of Westminster which had been destroyed by fire in 1834.

On William IV's death in 1837, Buckingham Palace passed to his successor, George III's granddaughter Victoria, who had just turned 18. Queen Victoria was the first monarch to live there, thus beginning its long tradition as the British royal residence.

Victoria married Prince Albert in 1840, and soon required more space to accommodate her growing family. The Marble Arch was moved to its current location at the north-east corner of Hyde Park, and in its place a fourth wing was constructed, thereby forming a quadrangle. The soft French stone that Blore had used on the eastern façade (the front facing the Mall) was deteriorating due to London's soot, and Sir Aston Webb was tasked with replacing it. He chose Portland Stone, and transformed the appearance of the palace into the building we recognize today.

The balcony took its first step into becoming an iconic part of royal tradition after Queen Victoria first used it to greet her subjects during celebrations for the Great Exhibition in 1851. A few years later when her daughter Princess Victoria was married, the balcony was used again by the royal family to acknowledge the crowds below. In 1914, George V was called out to reassure the public who were about to go to war; and on VE Day in 1945, Prime Minister Winston Churchill appeared alongside George VI and his wife, together with Princesses Elizabeth and Margaret. Today, the balcony is associated with royal weddings, Trooping the Colour (the sovereign's birthday), jubilee anniversaries of the monarch's coronation, and other national anniversaries such as the Battle of Britain.

The Royal Family on the balcony at following the marriage of the Duke and Duchess of Cambridge in May 2011.

Buckingham Palace is 355 feet in length, 390 feet deep and 80 feet high, and the interior occupies over 830,000 square feet of floorspace. There are 775 rooms, including 19 state rooms, 92 offices, 52 royal and guest bedrooms, 188 staff bedrooms and 78 bathrooms. There is even a post office, cinema, swimming pool, doctor's surgery and jeweller's workshop. Notable rooms include: the Ballroom, where State Banquets are held; the Music Room, where Prince Charles, Princess Anne, Prince Andrew and Prince William were christened; the Picture Gallery, containing magnificent paintings by Rembrandt, van Dyck, Canaletto, Rubens and Vermeer; the Throne

Room, for court gatherings, dancing and special occasions; the Belgian Suite, where foreign heads of state are entertained; and three Drawing Rooms – Green, Blue and White – featuring Sèvres porcelain, a Riesener desk and a gilded Erard piano. The White Drawing Room is used when guests are presented to the Queen (she enters via a hidden door disguised as a mirror and cabinet), as well as being the location for her annual televised Christmas speeches.

Outdoors, the garden is accessed via the Bow Room, through which some 50,000 invited guests pass each summer when attending one of the Queen's garden parties. The largest private garden in London, the park-like outdoor area covers 40 acres of land and includes a lake, helicopter landing area, tennis court, wisteria-covered summer house and the huge Waterloo Vase. Adjacent to the palace, the Royal Mews houses the Queen's coach horses, the

Below: *Buckingham Palace seen from the rear. Celebratory garden parties are held in the gardens.*

Right: *Queen Elizabeth II with then President of the US, Richard Nixon, on a state visit.*

Gold Stage Coach and other royal carriages.

Since 1993, much of Buckingham Palace has been open to the public during the summer months (late July until the end of September). Visitors can see the State Rooms, Picture Gallery, Grand Staircase and Throne Room, with many treasures on display – from fine art paintings and sculpture to porcelain and furniture. Throughout the year, the colourful spectacle of the Changing of the Guard occurs daily at 11:30am from April to July, and on alternate days in the other months. Finally, directly opposite Buckingham Palace sits the impressive memorial to Queen Victoria, a portrayal of the former queen surrounded by allegorical figures of Victory, Endurance, Courage, Truth, Justice, Science, Art and Agriculture – one of London's most popular backdrops for photographs.

Clarence House

A British royal home and one of the last surviving aristocratic townhouses in London, Clarence House is the official residence of Their Royal Highnesses the Prince of Wales and the Duchess of Cornwall.

The four-storey house was commissioned by Prince William Henry, Duke of Clarence (George III's third son) as a home for him and his wife Adelaide, as he found the adjacent Tudor-style St James's Palace too small. It was designed by John Nash – who was simultaneously remodelling Buckingham Palace – to fit into the south-west corner of St James's. Built in 1825–27, the house was a classically proportioned mansion faced in light-coloured stucco. Compared to Buckingham Palace, the interior was plain and informal, the only ornamental plasterwork being in the first-floor reception rooms, hung with crimson damask.

The Duke of Clarence was crowned King William IV, and upon his death in 1837 the house passed briefly to his sister, and then in 1840 to Princess Victoria of Saxe-Coburg-Saalfeld (Queen Victoria's mother). Victoria's second son Alfred lived there until his death in 1900, then her third son Arthur used the house until his death in 1942.

Clarence House was damaged during the Blitz (1940–41) and became the headquarters for the Red Cross and St John Ambulance Brigade for the remainder of World War II. In 1947, Princess Elizabeth and her new husband Prince Philip, Duke of Edinburgh, took up residence, and their children Charles, Anne, Andrew and Edward grew up there.

When George VI died suddenly in 1952 and Princess Elizabeth acceded to the throne the following year, the new queen and her family moved to Buckingham Palace while her mother Elizabeth and sister Margaret moved into Clarence House. The Queen Mother lived at Clarence House for 50 years, until her death in 2002.

After a year of exterior works and major interior refurbishment and redecoration, Prince Charles and his wife-to-be Camilla took up residence, keeping almost all of the Queen Mother's furniture but changing the colour schemes, adding to the art collection and planting a formal garden in her memory. Clarence House was home to Princes William and Harry too, before their marriages, and the Morning Room was the location for the official christening photograph of William and Catherine's second son Louis in 2018.

The grand stucco exterior of Clarence House, one of the grandest residences on a street of magnificent buildings.

Kensington Palace

The birthplace of Queen Victoria and currently the residence of the Duke and Duchess of Cambridge and their children, Kensington Palace has been home to young royals since the 17th century. The first version of Kensington Palace – then known as Nottingham House – was a two-storey mansion built in 1605 and purchased by Heneage Finch, 1st Earl of Nottingham. When William III and Mary II jointly ascended the throne in 1689, they bought the house and instructed the acclaimed English architect Christopher Wren to expand the existing design. The King's and Queen's Apartments were added and the house was re-oriented to face west. A *cour d'honneur* (three-sided ceremonial courtyard) was built at the entrance, so that visitors arrived through an

archway adorned with a clock tower. Lawns, formal gardens and flower beds completed the exterior Dutch-style layout. The King and Queen moved in by Christmas 1689, and from then onwards Kensington Palace became a residence for British monarchs.

In 1702, Queen Anne asked Christopher Wren to finish the designs he had started. He focused on the Queen's Apartments, building the Queen's Entrance and adding a gently sloping staircase between the private living area and the gardens, allowing Anne to walk outside gracefully. An Orangery was built by Nicholas Hawksmoor, and

Above: *The Drawing Room, dating from the era of William and Mary, was the focal point of court life.*

Below: *The façade of Kensington Palace, with a statue of young Queen Victoria.*

Above: *The elaborate Cupola Room, designed by Richard Cattermole in 1817.*

Right: *Kensington Palace with a statue of William III (of Orange) in the foreground. It was presented to Edward VII in 1907.*

then the young John Vanbrugh added elegant carvings and pillars.

Anne's successor George I commissioned three new State Rooms – the Cupola Room, Privy Chamber and Withdrawing Room – and the King's Staircase. William Kent decorated the rooms with elaborately gilded *trompe l'oeil* ceilings and walls, and painted the walls around the King's Staircase with a series of colourful and interesting Georgian characters. He also filled the palace with art and fine furniture, much of which remains today.

George II and his wife Queen Caroline took the lead in hosting sparkling receptions and intellectual gatherings for the brightest scientists and artists of the day. She hired Charles Bridgeman as royal gardener, and he designed the Serpentine boating lake, Round Pond and Broad Walk.

When George III became king in 1760, he bought Buckingham House and moved there, so Kensington Palace was used as a home for other royals. George III's sixth son, Prince Augustus Frederick, Duke of Sussex, moved into what became known as Apartment 1. The Duke's passion for the arts and sciences led to the construction of an enormous 10-room library filled more than 50,000 volumes and ornate 18th-century clocks.

The next resident was Prince Edward, Duke of Kent and Strathearn, whose daughter

Alexandrina Victoria – the future Queen Victoria – was born there in 1819 and grew up there. Later several minor royals took up residence, causing the palace to be nicknamed the 'Aunt Heap'. Victoria opened the State Apartments to the public in 1899, and in 1908, the ornamental Sunken Garden was planted.

During World War I George V allowed a number of rooms to be reserved for Irish prisoners and soldiers, and then the Queen's Apartments sustained bomb damage during the Blitz of 1940. In 1947 Prince Philip and Princess Elizabeth stayed there, and in the 1960s Princess Margaret and her husband the Earl of Snowdon lived in Apartment 10, and then the much larger Apartment 1A.

Following their wedding in 1981, Prince Charles and Princess Diana made their home at Kensington Palace, raising their sons William and Harry there. After her divorce, Diana continued to live in the palace until her death in 1997 and the Memorial Fountain was created in her memory. In 2013 the Duke and Duchess of Cambridge, William and Catherine, set up home in Apartment 1A. The Sunken Garden was chosen as the location for Prince Harry and Meghan Markle's engagement photocall in November 2017.

Kew Palace

A royal retreat hidden within the Royal Botanic Gardens at Kew on the banks of the River Thames, Kew Palace was once a large complex of buildings but now consists of just a few survivors, the main one being the red-brick Dutch House. The kitchens have been preserved as they were 200 years ago, and they are open to the public.

The smallest of all the British royal palaces, the Dutch House was originally built on top of the undercroft of an earlier building for the successful and wealthy Flemish silk merchant Samuel Fortrey in 1631. Fortrey's family came from Lille in northern France, but confusion over his ancestry combined with the distinctive architectural

style (large Dutch gables) led to the title of 'Dutch House'. Over the entrance of the house, Fortrey built a lover's knot containing the initials 'S' and 'C', for Samuel and his wife Catherine.

When King George II and Queen Caroline came to the throne in 1727, they chose the Dutch House as a residence for their three eldest daughters, as well as taking on leases for several nearby properties. The location was suitably private, where the young royals could enjoy normal lives in tranquil surroundings. George and Caroline's son Frederick, Prince of Wales, lived opposite in a building called the White House (no longer standing, but marked by a sundial in Kew Gardens). Frederick developed the gardens (which became the Royal Botanic Gardens, Kew) and added a new kitchen block called the Royal Kitchens. These kitchens were hubs of frenzied activity throughout the 1730s, with around 30 cooks preparing the royal meals. In 1818, the kitchens were closed and the doors were locked, so visitors today are able to have an authentic glimpse into 18th-century domestic life as it was then, from the original elm table in the middle of the room to the enormous fireplace with a smokejack and spit racks.

Above: *The Queen's Drawing Room, restored to its 18th century form with carefully researched paint colours.*

Left: *The back of Kew Palace with its elegant and fragrant formal garden.*

After Frederick died in 1751, his widow Augusta continued living in the White House, and the Dutch House was turned into a schoolhouse for her two eldest

sons, George (the future George III) and Edward. In due course, George III sent his own sons to the same schoolhouse – giving rise to its nickname of 'the Prince of Wales's House' – and meanwhile he began filling the White House with a valuable art collection, including works by Canaletto and Johann Zoffany.

In 1788, George III experienced his first bout of 'madness'. Initially, he was incarcerated in the White House while his wife Charlotte and their other daughters stayed in the Dutch House. Doctors worked tirelessly to try to cure the king, administering emetics and laxatives, giving him freezing baths and even making him wear a straitjacket. He recovered briefly but soon suffered recurrences. As his condition worsened, George was moved into the Dutch House and then finally Windsor Castle. The empty White House fell into disrepair and was demolished in 1802.

The Dutch House was used as a venue for the double wedding of George and Charlotte's sons

William and Edward in 1818, and Charlotte died there in her bedroom later that year, too unwell to make it back home to Windsor. She lay in state in the dining room before being transported to Windsor for burial. George III died at Windsor two years later.

The next king, George IV, demolished the Castellated Palace and had plans to demolish the Dutch House too, but it was saved by his brother William IV. William offered the house to his sister Victoria and her daughter, the future Queen Victoria, but she declined because she deemed it too old and too devoid of furniture.

In the summer of 1844, Queen Victoria sent three of her children to the Dutch House, but thereafter it was unoccupied and the stables and much of the service wing demolished. In 1898, to mark her Diamond Jubilee, Queen Victoria gave the house to Kew Gardens.

In 1969, a replica 17th-century Dutch garden was planted at the back of the house. Extensive restoration work was carried out in the late 1990s, and in 2006 Charles, Prince of Wales, threw a lavish party and fireworks display to celebrate Queen Elizabeth II's 80th birthday. Kew Palace was reopened to the public in the summer months. Highlights include the Royal Kitchens, Madame Tussaud's bust of George III, the Princesses' Bedrooms, Queen Charlotte's chair and the Pagoda in the gardens.

Left: *The exquisitely manicured formal gardens at the back of the palace with their high and low hedging and statuary.*

Right: *The Dutch influences on the palace include the rounded gables seen here.*

Eltham Palace

Eltham Palace is a unique combination of medieval palace, Tudor residence and Art Deco mansion. Dating back to 1305, the manor was given to Edward II by the Bishop of Durham, Anthony Bek. Edward added a new wall around Bek's original wall and moat, with buttresses to support the original masonry. By the 14th century, Eltham Palace had become one of the largest royal residences in England, and alterations included a new drawbridge, service buildings, royal lodgings and a bathroom with a tiled floor and glazed windows. The land beyond the moat – about 1,300 acres – was enclosed to form the Great Park.

Throughout the 14th, 15th and 16th centuries, many monarchs lived at Eltham Palace. Edward IV built the magnificent Great Hall in the 1470s, and Henry VIII grew up there though once he turned his attention to Hampton Court Palace and Greenwich, Eltham fell into disrepair.

The palace was used as a farm for some time. A few repairs were made during the 19th century,

Left: *Art Deco style at its finest in the entrance hall to the 1930s addition to the palace.*

Right: *The warm brick and stone façade of the old house.*

and the Great Hall was used for entertaining and as an indoor tennis court.

Then in 1933, Stephen and Virginia Courtauld acquired the lease, transforming the palace into an idiosyncratic mixture of old and new. The exterior was designed in a retro 'Wrenaissance' style, and the interior showcased their personal tastes with an eclectic mixture of Art Deco, fashionable ocean-liner style and Swedish modernism. Old Masters were hung next to contemporary paintings, and electric fires, loudspeakers and underfloor heating were installed – including a bespoke heated room for the Courtauld's pet lemur, Mah-Jongg. Outdoors, they created a rock garden, formal rose gardens and a series of Edwardian-style garden 'rooms'.

Today, visitors can explore the lavish lifestyle of the Courtaulds and their high-tech home as well as their travels around the world.

Witley Court

Formerly one of the greatest stately homes of England, in its heyday Witley Court was staffed by over 100 servants and was the setting for glamorous parties and extravagant royal entertainments. A major fire in 1937 caused severe damage, and the house lost its roof and was emptied of its fittings and furnishings. However, the spectacular ruins remain intact and are open to the public.

Located in Great Witley, Worcestershire, the estate was originally bought by the ironmaster Thomas Foley in the 17th century, and his descendants added towers, two wings, a lake and a chapel. The interior of the chapel was decorated with panels painted by Antonio Bellucci, as well as beautiful hand-painted windows.

In the early 19th century, just when the Foley fortunes were

running out, Thomas Foley VII made an advantageous marriage and hired the top Regency architect, John Nash, to expand the house, adding two enormous porticos. Then Witley Court was sold to the trustees of the teenage William Ward, 1st Earl of Dudley, in 1833. Ward made a fortune from the coal industry and decided to commission the architect Samuel Daukes to remodel the house. The exterior was recast in Bath stone in the ornate Italianate style that had been used at Osborne House for Queen Victoria and Prince Albert. Another new wing was added, this time with a magnificent glass-roofed conservatory.

The scale and magnificence of Witley Court is still apparent as it presides over the formal gardens and great fountain.

At its peak, Witley Court was furnished in the style of Louis XV and a veritable army of servants was employed there. The gardens were matching in grandeur, with beautiful formal parterres and a magnificent fountain built by the leading garden designer of the day, William Andrews Nesfield.

A terrible fire broke out in 1937, and within the space of a single night the house was reduced to a shell of smoking ruins. It was never occupied again, but English Heritage subsequently restored the gardens to their former Victorian glory. The Perseus and Andromeda fountain is in working order and is said to be one of Europe's greatest. Between April and October, it fires dramatic jets of water on the hour.

Chartwell

Famous as the family home of Winston Churchill, Chartwell is a Victorian country house near Westerham in Kent. It contains many of Churchill's personal possessions and treasures, including many of his own paintings. The National Trust acquired the house in 1946 – and Winston and his wife Clementine continued to live there – and the rooms, art studio and gardens have been lovingly preserved.

The estate dates back to 1362 when the Tudor property (known as Well Street) belonged to William-at-Well. It is said that Henry VIII stayed there while courting Anne Boleyn. In 1848, it was sold to the former MP John Campbell Colquhoun,

Above: *Winston Churchill in his study at Chartwell.*
Left: *Though large, Chartwell has a homely and domestic feel to it.*

who rebuilt and enlarged the original farmhouse, and renamed it 'Chartwell'.

The property remained in the Colquhoun family until 1922, when Winston Churchill bought it to use as a base during the 1920s and 30s. Clementine was worried about the cost of living there, but Winston wrote to her in 1923: 'My beloved, I beg you not to worry about money, or to feel insecure. Chartwell is to be our home [and] we must endeavour to live there for many years.' The following year, he wrote again to his wife: 'This is the first letter I have ever written from this place, and it is right that it should be to you.' As well as being a talented artist, Churchill was an amateur bricklayer, and he constructed several buildings and garden walls at Chartwell.

The years 1922–1939 were happy and busy at Chartwell. Churchill invited many work colleagues to visit him, and enjoyed late-night evenings talking about battle tactics enacted with decanters and wine glasses as props, and cigar smoke to represent gun fire.

During World War II, Chartwell was left mostly vacant while Churchill served as Prime Minister in London (1940–45), although he did return at times of high stress – he spent the night at Chartwell before the fall of France in 1940, and another night there in 1941 after the failure of Operation Battleaxe to relieve Tobruk.

After the war and his election loss in 1945, Churchill returned

Above: *Oscar Nemon's statue of Winston and Clementine Churchill at Chartwell.*

Right: *Lavender and roses line the golden rose walk, created by the Churchills' children for their parents in 1958.*

to Chartwell. The following year he asked his architect to convert the summer house into a butterfly house, and raised caterpillars and chrysalises to breed butterflies. He planted the garden with nectar-rich flowering shrubs, such as buddleja and lavender, to encourage them.

Churchill returned to London as Prime Minister (1951–55), but he was ageing and increasingly unwell. He was forced to retire when he suffered a stroke in 1955, and he returned to Chartwell for the final decade of his life. He made a remarkable recovery for a while, allowing him enough time to complete the sixth and final volume of his war memoirs.

The National Trust opened Chartwell to the public in 1966, and it became an instant success. The house is shown as it was in the 1930s, when Winston, Clementine and their four children were living there.

The top floor has a museum and a series of uniform rooms, each reflecting a particular era. The rest of the house consists of: the sitting room with Churchill's prize-winning landscape painting entitled *Winter Sunshine, Chartwell*; the drawing room where Churchill played the card game Bezique with his guests; the library where Churchill liked to escape to get some quiet work done; Lady Churchill's bedroom painted in duck egg blue, with a photograph of daughter Marigold who died aged two, and also one of the last-ever photographs of Winston; the study – known as 'the heart of Chartwell' – where Churchill spent hours standing at the large mahogany desk planning his budgets as Chancellor of the Exchequer and writing speeches warning against the rise of Hitler; and the dining room with its circular weathered oak table, bright green chintz curtains and arched French windows.

The gardens are also open to the public, and visitors can enjoy the atmospheric landscape that Winston and Clementine loved so dearly, with lakes and ponds that he helped to create, the vegetable garden enclosed by the brick wall he built himself, and the 'Marycot' playhouse that he designed for his youngest daughter Mary.

Knole

Situated in a 1,000-acre medieval deer park south-east of Sevenoaks in Kent, Knole is said to be in the top five of England's largest houses. Visitors have been coming to Knole for 400 years to see its many world-class paintings and an important collection of 17th-century furniture.

Dating back to the 1290s, the estate was originally owned by Robert de Knole. Much building work was done over the following centuries: it was extended and occupied by several Archbishops of Canterbury from 1456 onwards, and became a royal household during the Tudor era. Henry VIII was fond of hunting deer at Knole.

Henry's daughter Elizabeth I passed the estate to her cousin, Thomas Sackville, 1st Earl of Dorset: thirteen generations of the

Sackville family have owned or lived in the property ever since. From 1603, its showrooms have been used to display the Sackvilles' impressive treasures. These include Stuart furniture, fine tapestries, the Knole Settee (on which the monarch would sit while receiving visitors) and valuable portraits by Van Dyke, Gainsborough and Sir Joshua Reynolds, to name a few. A private chapel houses an oak organ with foot-pumped bellows, thought to be the oldest playable organ in England, dating from the early 1620s.

Above: *The deer park at Knole is home to both fallow and red deer such as this splendid stag.*

Left: *Knole's impressive frontage is extremely well preserved and coherent in its style.*

One fascinating resident of Knole was the writer Vita Sackville-West, who was born, grew up and married there, and became the partner and muse of Virginia Woolf. Woolf's novel *Orlando* (1928) was based on Vita's gender-fluid life – Vita was a free spirit and frequently dressed as a man.

The design of the house is sometimes described as a 'Calendar House', so named because it was thought to contain 365 rooms, 52 staircases, 12 entrances and 7 courtyards. It is difficult to prove this, however, because it depends on how the rooms are counted. At any rate, many of the rooms have been perfectly preserved, making Knole a uniquely precious Jacobean home based on a medieval archbishop's palace.

Petworth House

Nestled in the South Downs of West Sussex, Petworth House is a late 17th-century manor house containing a wonderful collection of fine art, and Emery Molyneux's original terrestrial globe. The 700-acre deer park contains the biggest fallow deer herd in England. The site was chosen in the 14th century by Henry de Percy, and it remained in the Percy family, the Earls of Northumberland, for generations.

When Josceline Percy, the 11th Earl, died in 1670, his sole heir – a two-year-old daughter, Elizabeth, inherited everything. She was married twice by the age of 16, but her third marriage lasted, and she

Left: *Various coats of arms on display on a stained glass window.*

Below: *Charles' Seymour's Baroque redevelopment of Petworth seen from across the lake.*

and her husband Charles Seymour, 6th Duke of Somerset, became one of the richest couples in England.

In 1688, Seymour rebuilt the house in the Baroque style, inspired by the Palace of Versailles and other grand royal palaces in Europe. His ambitious plans for Petworth included a magnificent west front and exquisite marble hall. He and his wife were among Queen Anne's closest friends.

A few years after Seymour's death, 'Capability' Brown was commissioned to design the gardens. He replaced the formal layouts with a deer park and a naturalistic Pleasure Ground, with wooded paths and far-reaching views of the South Downs.

Seymour's descendant George O'Brien Wyndham, 3rd Earl of Egremont, inherited the estate in 1763. A keen art collector, he was a patron to many artists of the time, including John Constable and J.M.W. Turner, who created a panoramic painting of it, *Petworth House from the Lake: Dewy Morning* (*c.* 1810). In addition to paintings, Wyndham also collected ornate wood carvings, many of which are by Grinling Gibbons, Britain's greatest wood carver.

Petworth House was given to the nation in 1947 and is now managed by the National Trust. It is home to an incredible collection of landscapes, sculptures, wall and ceiling paintings and wood carvings, and the house has appeared in films such as *Elizabeth: The Golden Age* (2007), Mr Turner (2014) and *Maleficent* (2014).

Polesden Lacey

Set on the North Downs at Great Bookham, near Dorking, Surrey, Polesden Lacey contains a fine collection of paintings, furniture, porcelain and silver, as well as 1,400 acres of gardens.

The name 'Polesden' is believed to be Saxon, and the first house on the site was built in 1336. This was demolished and rebuilt several times during the 19th century, then bought in 1902 by a civil servant, Sir Clinton Edward Dawkins. He commissioned the architect Ambrose Poynter to make adjustments to the building but died before their completion.

The estate was then purchased by Scottish politician and brewer William McEwan for his daughter Margaret and her husband, the Conservative politician Ronald 'Ronnie' Greville. Margaret turned out to be the daughter of one of

McEwan's brewery employees, but nevertheless became a respected socialite and unassailable owner of Polesden Lacey for the next 36 years, from 1906 to 1942.

Mrs Greville and Ronnie made a good match. She had money and he royal connections – he was heir to a baronetcy and mixed in royal social circles, including that of the future King Edward VII. They employed the architects of the Ritz Hotel in London, Mewès and Davis, to renovate the house and the result was a neoclassical exterior and a decadent Edwardian interior.

Polesden Lacey became the venue for lavish parties attended by Prime Ministers, heads of state and celebrities. The rooms were filled with velvet furnishings, gilt mirrors, exquisite porcelain and silver, and the walls hung with portraits by British artists such as Raeburn, Lawrence and Reynolds, including a painting of Mrs Greville. A wall rose garden, lawns, ancient woodlands and landscape walks completed the scene.

Sadly, Ronnie died just two years after buying the house, but Mrs Greville became one of the most famous hostesses of the early 20th century. When she invited the Duke and Duchess of York (later George VI and Queen Elizabeth) to spend their honeymoon at Polesden Lacey in 1923, they accepted gladly, and the house appeared in every newspaper in the land. In 1942, it was left to the National Trust.

The elegant façade and sweeping lawns of Polesden Lacey on an autumn day.

Osborne House

A palatial home in East Cowes on the Isle of Wight, Osborne House was Queen Victoria and Prince Albert's seaside retreat. It is elaborately decorated in the Italian Renaissance style, designed by Prince Albert himself and built by Thomas Cubitt (whose company designed the front of Buckingham Palace). Victoria died there in 1901.

The first Osborne House was owned by the Blachford family in 1705, and consisted of a three-storey Georgian residence with a brick stable block and a walled kitchen garden. In 1843, the Prime Minister, Sir Robert Peel, recommended the estate to Queen Victoria and Prince Albert, who were in the market for a summer home to escape the stresses of royal court life. The views of the Solent were reminiscent of the Bay of Naples, and Victoria asserted: 'It is impossible to imagine a prettier

The gardens at Osborne House present an ever-changing picture through the year, the planting adjusted to each season.

Above: *The State Dining Room at Osborne House with its ornate ceiling.*

Right: *A colourized postcard of Osborne house taken c.1890–1900, during the last years of Queen Victoria's reign.*

spot.' Victoria and Albert leased the estate from Lady Isabella Blachford in 1844, then bought it in 1845 for £28,000.

The house was too small for the royal couple's needs, so Albert commissioned the talented master builder Thomas Cubitt to create an entirely new structure. The first phase of building was a Pavilion containing the private apartments of Victoria and Albert, with nurseries for their expanding family, a billiard room, dining room and drawing room. Next, a household wing was built to accommodate members of the royal household, and finally a main wing replaced the site of the old house and was linked to the house by a long corridor. This last wing was designed by John Lockwood Kipling, father of Rudyard, and features the renowned Durbar Room (from the Hindi word *durbar* meaning 'court'), created for Victoria's youngest daughter, Beatrice, and decorated in a highly intricate Indian style. Other additions included a timber Swiss Cottage for the education of the royal children (a mile east of the house) and a stable big enough to house 50 horses and carriages.

Tragedy struck in 1861 with the sudden death of Prince Albert at Windsor Castle, but Victoria continued to visit Osborne for the rest of her life. Her wish was that the house remain in the family, but when no one wanted to claim it, it was given to the state.

During World War II, some parts of the house were used for convalescing soldiers, with famous patients including the author of *Winnie-the-Pooh*, A.A. Milne, and the historical writer Robert Graves.

Today, Osborne House is managed by English Heritage, and guests are able to stay at a holiday cottage in the grounds, with access to Victoria and Albert's private beach. As a tribute to Queen Victoria, Government House in Victoria, Australia, is a copy of Osborne House.

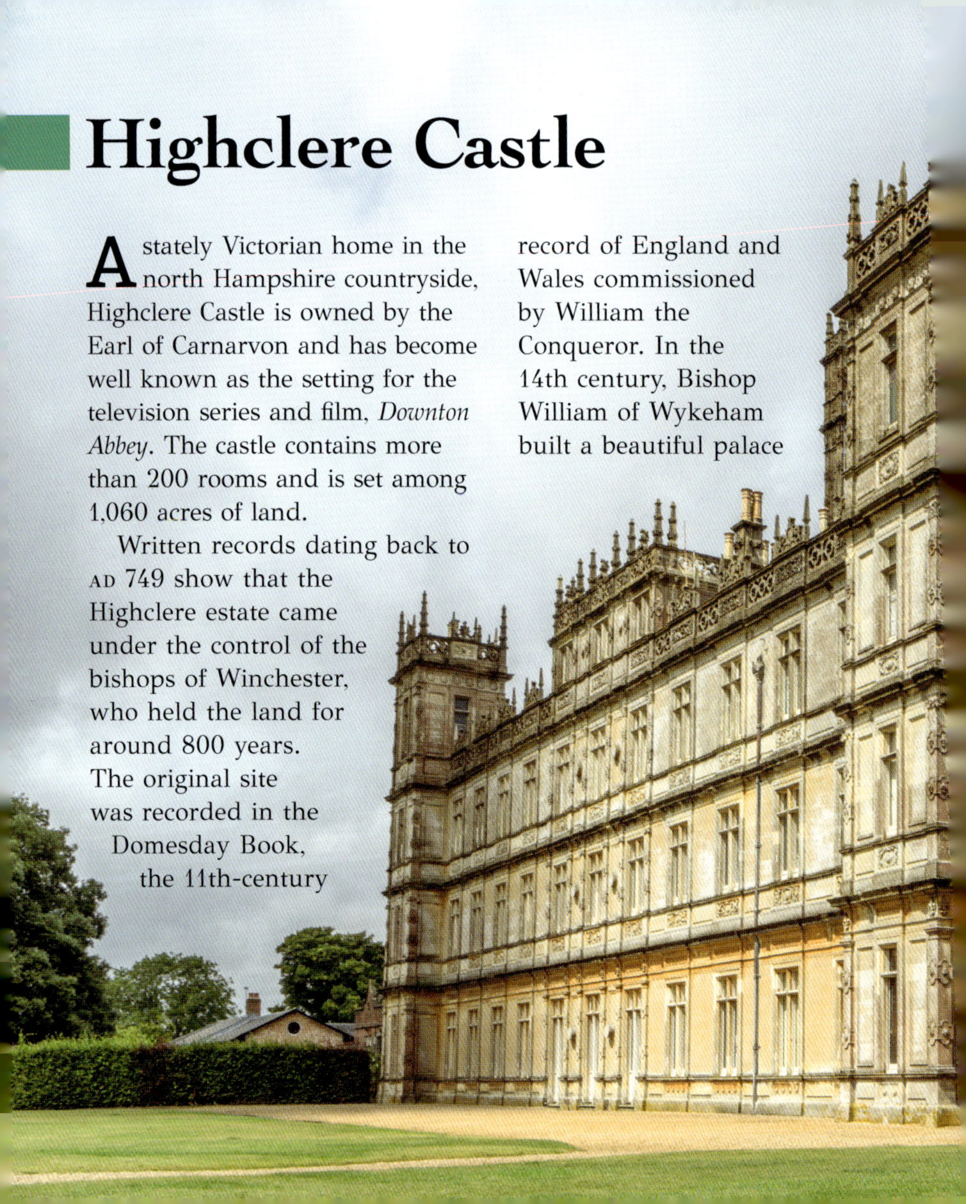

Highclere Castle

A stately Victorian home in the north Hampshire countryside, Highclere Castle is owned by the Earl of Carnarvon and has become well known as the setting for the television series and film, *Downton Abbey*. The castle contains more than 200 rooms and is set among 1,060 acres of land.

Written records dating back to AD 749 show that the Highclere estate came under the control of the bishops of Winchester, who held the land for around 800 years. The original site was recorded in the Domesday Book, the 11th-century record of England and Wales commissioned by William the Conqueror. In the 14th century, Bishop William of Wykeham built a beautiful palace and gardens for himself on the grounds, but this was confiscated by Edward VI in 1551 during the Protestant Reformation.

Several owners occupied Highclere over the next century and a quarter, until 1679 when the palace was purchased by Sir Robert Sawyer, politician and future Attorney General to Charles II and James II. Sawyer – who is a direct ancestor of the current Earl of Carnarvon – rebuilt the house, and his descendants added follies such as Heaven's Gate and Jackdaw's Castle, as well as constructing paths and formal gardens and starting a collection of portraits.

The view of Highclere Castle that many viewers will recall from the opening credits of Downton Abbey, the series that made the house famous.

Left: *An aerial view of Highclere Castle.*

Right: *The saloon at Highclere shows the scale and detail of the castle's interior.*

Henry Herbert, himself a descendant of Sawyer, inherited Highclere and was made the 1st Earl of Carnarvon in 1793. He hired the famous landscape gardener Lancelot 'Capability' Brown to oversee changes to the grounds, and Brown's improvements included the planting of many trees (including cedars of Lebanon, oaks, beeches, elms and ashes), altering the landscape to give it a more natural appearance, and moving the remains of the village church into a corner of the castle.

The most significant changes to the house were made by the 3rd Earl, who commissioned Sir Charles Barry in 1838 to remodel the house completely. Barry had recently designed the Palace of Westminster in London, and his opulent exterior and interior style transformed Highclere from a house into the magnificent mansion it is today. By 1842, Highclere had taken on a Jacobethan style, a combination of both Elizabethan and Jacobean architecture, with some Italianate motifs, exemplifying the Renaissance Revival movement of the time.

A few years later, Highclere Castle played a part in the foundation of Canada: the 4th Earl drafted the British North America Act of 1867, together with John A. Macdonald, who became the first Prime Minister of Canada.

At the start of the 20th century, Highclere began a long association with aviation history. Sir Geoffrey De Havilland made his first flight of a Tiger Moth there in 1910, airmen and soldiers were treated as patients throughout World War I, and during World War II many military planes crashed on the estate while on active service.

Highclere commemorates its wartime history in a tranquil part of the garden that contains a cedar wood airman statue surrounded by benches made from the shrapnel of crashed planes, and inside the castle the names of World War II evacuees are etched into the roof lead.

Another point of historical interest is that the 5th Earl of Carnarvon, together with his friend Howard Carter, travelled to Egypt's Valley of the Kings in 1922, where they discovered Tutankhamen's Tomb – spawning the explosion of interest in ancient Egypt.

The castle opened to the public in 1988, and is home to the 8th Earl and Countess of Carnarvon. As well as being the location for *Downton Abbey* (2010–15 and 2019), Highclere was used in *The Missionary* (1982), *The Secret Garden* (1987), *A Handful of Dust* (1988), *Jeeves and Wooster* (1990–93), *Robin Hood: Prince of Thieves* (1991) and *Eyes Wide Shut* (1999).

Beaulieu Palace House

Pronounced 'Bewly', this 13th-century Gothic country house set in the heart of the New Forest in Beaulieu, Hampshire, was originally the gatehouse of Beaulieu Abbey, and the site is now home to Britain's National Motor Museum.

The history of Beaulieu Abbey dates back to 1203 when it was founded by King John. Henry VIII dissolved the monasteries in 1538, at which point Thomas Wriothesley, 1st Earl of Southampton, bought the abbey and its surrounding estate. Southhampton demolished the church but converted the porch, hall and chapels into the manor house we see today. He also preserved the refectory, cloisters and dormitory, and the house is still owned by his descendants, the Barons Montagu of Beaulieu.

The 3rd Baron of Montagu, Edward Douglas-Scott-Montagu, was something of an entrepreneur, and had noticed in the 1950s that stately homes around the country were struggling to survive, so he decided to open the house to the public and display his family treasures, portraits, antique car collection and gardens. He also loved jazz music, and staged the first country jazz festival in the palace grounds.

In 1952 his car exhibition consisted of just a few examples parked in his front hall, but these became so popular with the public that by 1972 he had a collection of 300 cars. He decided to house them in a purpose-built museum in the parklands, and thus founded the world-famous National Motor Museum.

The museum has one of the finest collections of cars, motorcycles and motoring memorabilia in the world. Exhibitions have included James Bond's vehicles and 'On Screen

Cars', featuring Del Boy's Reliant Regal from *Only Fools and Horses* and Mr Bean's lime green Mini, as well as a permanent exhibit showcasing the BBC's *World of Top Gear*.

Beaulieu Palace House is said to be one of the most haunted houses in Britain. Sir Arthur Conan Doyle participated in a séance there, and the ghost of the Countess of Beaulieu, Lady Isabella, has reportedly been sighted walking through walls.

Beaulieu's origins as an abbey are still apparent in the shape of many windows and other details.

Blenheim Palace

Located in Woodstock, Oxfordshire, Blenheim Palace is one of the largest houses in England, and is considered a true national treasure. Its story began with the 1704 Battle of Blenheim in Bavaria, after which Queen Anne gifted a large plot of hunting land to John Churchill, 1st Duke of Marlborough, for his victory there against Louis XIV (and for other victories during the War of the Spanish Succession).

Construction began in 1705 under the guidance of architect John Vanbrugh, whose flamboyant design of Castle Howard in Yorkshire had greatly impressed the Duke of Marlborough. The Duchess of Marlborough, however, did not agree with her husband. She favoured the designer of St Paul's Cathedral instead – Sir Christopher Wren – and expressed her displeasure by questioning every decision along the way. Criticisms of design, taste, extravagance and cost caused the building process to be painfully long and drawn out, the final palace not being completed until 1722.

The English Baroque styling of Blenheim Palace is couched in the golden stone of the local area.

Above: *Blenheim's First State Room, with paintings, tapestry and fine furniture.*

Right: The Triumph of the Duke of Marlborough *depicted on the Saloon ceiling c.1720 by Louis Laguerre.*

Once finished, however, Blenheim Palace became famous as an outstanding example of English Baroque architecture, sitting within a large walled garden and surrounded by more than 2,000 acres of parkland. The gardens went on to be modified by Lancelot 'Capability' Brown in 1764: he transformed the parkland by damming the canal that flowed under Vanbrugh's Grand Bridge so that it produced a naturalistic serpentine lake – thus achieving his trademark view of a house seen beyond a stretch of reflective water.

A century later, Blenheim Palace became home to Sir Winston Churchill, a direct descendant of the Dukes of Marlborough – he was born there in 1874. He became a close friend of the 9th Duke and proposed to his wife Clementine Hozier in the Temple of Diana, and his life and times are commemorated by a permanent exhibition open to the public.

By the end of the 19th century, the palace received a much-needed injection of money; fortuitously the 9th Duke of Marlborough married the American railroad heiress Consuelo Vanderbilt and used her fortune to restore the palace to its former glory. During World War I, the palace was used as a convalescent hospital for wounded soldiers, and in World War II, it was used as a base by MI5. In 1987, Blenheim Palace was designated a UNESCO World Heritage Site, and is currently home to Charles James

Spencer-Churchill, 12th Duke of Marlborough.

Visitors can see some of the finest antique collections in Europe – the State Rooms contain exquisite portraits, tapestries and furniture – as well as stunning examples of Baroque architecture. Blenheim Palace is also a venue for weddings and banqueting events, a film and television location, and even a producer of its own brand of mineral water.

Outside, there are beautiful walks up to the Grand Cascades or around the lake, with Pleasure Gardens (including a giant hedge maze and butterfly house), Formal Gardens (including the Water Terraces, Rose Garden, Secret Garden and the Duke's Italian Garden), historical monuments such as the Column of Victory, Grand Bridge and Temple of Diana, a miniature train and an adventure playground.

The area of the estate known as High Park is home to the largest collection of ancient oak trees in Europe, many of which are over 400 years old, and some even date back to AD 970. Horticulturalists and Harry Potter fans alike travel from all over the world to see the magnificent 300-year-old cedar of Lebanon tree which stands alone by the lake, where scenes for *Harry Potter and the Order of the Phoenix* (2007) were filmed. Other trees are even older, such as the 900-year-old 'King Oak'.

Other productions filmed at Blenheim Palace include *Greystoke: The Legend of Tarzan, Lord of the Apes* (1984), *Entrapment* (1999), *The Young Victoria* (2009), *Gulliver's Travels* (2010), the television series *The Royals* (2015), *Cinderella* (2015), *Mission Impossible: Rogue Nation* (2015), *Spectre* (2015), *The BFG* (2016) and *Transformers: The Last Knight* (2017).

Blenheim's maze in the Pleasure Gardens, a few minutes walk from the house, is more than two miles in length.

Stonor Park

One of the oldest family homes still inhabited today, Stonor Park is a Tudor country house and private deer park nestled in the Chiltern Hills at Stonor in Oxfordshire. It is the ancestral home of the Stonor family – the Barons Camoys – going back more than eight centuries, and contains a beautiful collection of portraits, tapestries, bronzes and ceramics. There is also a 14th-century chapel, and the grounds include Italianate gardens with stunning views of the surrounding hills and woods.

The original site of the house was a prehistoric stone circle, hence the name. The remains of

the circle are still visible today, as they were moved a slight distance away when the gardens were landscaped.

The red-brick house and chapel are thought to have been built around 1280, when Sir Richard Stonor married his second wife Margaret Harnhull. Many additions and renovations were made over the next three centuries, including the adoption of the E-shaped design in 1540.

During the English Reformation, when Henry VIII formed the Church of England, the Stonor family remained loyal to the Pope and the Roman Catholic Church. They reduced their public role but took in recusants – people who refused to attend Anglican services. One such person was the Jesuit priest Edmund Campion, who lived and worked at Stonor in 1581. Under threat of death, he covertly printed a pamphlet called *Decem Rationes* (Ten Reasons) on a printing press at Stonor. It set forth ten arguments against Protestantism. Very soon afterwards, Campion was captured, taken to the Tower of London, convicted of treason and executed. Centuries later, however, he was beatified (1886) and then canonized (1970). Visitors to Stonor Park can see the roof space and priest hole where he hid during his time there.

The Stonors remained faithful Catholics throughout the 17th and 18th centuries, and locals were able to attend mass in the private chapel. A fortuitous upshot of the marginalization of the family is that the house remained well preserved and unchanged.

Regularly used in feature films, television series and commercials, Stonor Park has appeared in *The Living Daylights* (1987), the movie version of Roald Dahl's *Danny, the Champion of the World* (1989) and the TV series *Midsomer Murders* (1997), *Endeavour* (2019) and *A Christmas Carol* (2019).

Stonor House in its peaceful setting in the Chiltern Hills .

Hampton Court Palace

Situated on the River Thames in the borough of Richmond upon Thames, Hampton Court Palace was built in the early 16th century and was home to Henry VIII and all six of his wives. In the 17th century, William III and Mary II commissioned Christopher Wren to transform it into an elegant Baroque palace intended to rival Paris's Palace of Versailles. Queen Victoria opened it to the public in 1838, and its grand interiors, incredible art collection

and stunning formal gardens – including a famous maze as well as the annual Royal Horticultural Society's summer garden festival – attract millions of visitors each year.

From 1514, Cardinal Thomas Wolsey, Henry VIII's Lord Chancellor, poured enormous amounts of money into transforming what was originally an ordinary country house into a lavish Tudor palace – complete with a Royal Tennis Court – fit for a king. The architecture became a hybrid of English Gothic and Italian Renaissance classical style, and Henry VIII liked the result so much that he decided to live there himself.

Henry VIII added the Great Hall, where William Shakespeare's *Hamlet* and *Macbeth* were

Fountain Court, seen from the garden side, is a Baroque addition to the original Tudor palace.

performed in 1603, and expanded the Great Kitchens so that up to 800 courtiers could be served 1,600 meals per day. The gatehouse, later known as Anne Boleyn's Gate, was adorned with an astronomical clock showing times of the day, phases of the moon, zodiac signs and the tide level at London Bridge. It is said that the ghost of Henry's third wife Jane Seymour, who died in 1537 shortly after giving birth, still appears as a 'white wraith' at Hampton Court Palace on the anniversary of her death (24 October).

In 1689, William III and Mary II took the throne and made substantial changes to the palace, keeping much of the Tudor style but adding Baroque features. The pink brickwork combined

Right: *The Privy Chamber where King William would meet statesmen, ambassadors and other dignitaries*

Below: *The front of the palace retains its original Tudor characteristics.*

with pale Portland stone masonry blocks gave the building its highly distinctive look, and the addition of the Great Fountain (with yew trees left unclipped, as specified by Lancelot 'Capability' Brown), Privy Garden and Maze completed the design. The Maze was originally planted with hornbeam, then later replaced with more sturdy yew trees in the 1960s, but hornbeam is now being re-introduced.

Queen Anne commissioned Christopher Wren to return to Hampton Court to remodel the

Below: *A panelled corridor with elegant chequered marble floor.*

Right: *One of Hampton Court's sunken gardens with bright summer planting.*

chapel in 1710: a grand timber altar screen was placed over the brickwork, boxed-in pews were added and a new organ was installed. George I built new apartments for his son and daughter-in-law, George and Caroline (the Prince and Princess of Wales), and added a new kitchen, now known as the Georgian House. The architect William Kent brought in new furnishings and décor, decorating the walls of the Queen's Staircase with a *trompe l'oeil* dome with the star of the Order of the Garter in the centre.

King George II and Queen Caroline were the last monarchs to live at Hampton Court Palace, preferring Kensington Palace from the late 1730s onwards. Various aristocratic widows were granted residence, but the accommodation was cold and damp, and there was no hot water. Once the palace was opened to the public from 1838, throngs of visitors began arriving by boat, coach and railway to admire the spectacular architecture, try to find their way out of the maze or

watch a game of historic tennis.

One of the largest and most prestigious garden shows in the world, the RHS Hampton Court Palace Garden Festival (formerly Flower Show) has been running every July since 1993. The superb art collection contains many of the Royal Collection's finest works, and a new attraction called the Magic Garden – a children's playground filled with mythical beasts, battlements, towers and a secret grotto – was opened by the Duchess of Cambridge in 2016. The feature film *The Favourite* (2018), depicting the court of Queen Anne, was filmed in the Great Kitchens, the Cartoon Gallery and the Fountain Court.

CHAPTER 2

ENGLAND
South West

England's west country has a great variety of stately homes, just a few of which are showcased here. Some, such as Longleat in Wiltshire and Montacute in Somerset were built on a grand scale and use the full beauty of the local Cotswold stone throughout. Several have their origins in religious buildings that were abbeys or monasteries and whose names still recall that past – such as Lacock Abbey, pictured right. Saltram, in Devon is an early Georgian masterpiece decorated exquisitely by Robert Adam, while Tyntesfield was designed to be a home to a prosperous Victorian family but is also a brilliant example of that era's Gothic Revival architectural style.

The cloisters at Lacock Abbey are a remnant of its eccelsiastical past.

Lacock Abbey

Founded in the early 13th century by Ela, Countess of Salisbury, Lacock Abbey is a medieval country house in Lacock, Wiltshire. It holds the title of 'the birthplace of photography' because William Henry Fox Talbot lived there and created the earliest surviving photographic negative in 1835 – a picture of an oriel window in the abbey. More recently, it was used as a location in several Harry Potter movies: the cloisters and side rooms became classrooms at

Right: *The exquisitely detailed cloisters date from the 15th century and the house was built over them.*

Below: *Lacock Abbey's many stages of development can be clearly seen including its various styles of chimneys and windows.*

Hogwarts School of Witchcraft and Wizardry, and the Mirror of Erised was contained within.

Lacock Abbey functioned as an Augustinian nunnery from 1232 until the Dissolution of the Monasteries in the 16th century. The finely vaulted cloisters visible today were built in the 1400s (replacing the original cloisters), and the abbey was sold to Sir William Sharington, a courtier at the time of Henry VIII, for the sum of £783 in 1540. Sharington converted the building into a private residence, adding a three-storey octagonal tower, twisted Renaissance chimney stacks and an enclosed stable courtyard, but still retained many medieval features.

The house was fortified at the beginning of the English Civil War (1642) and Royalist troops protected it from the Parliamentarian 'Roundheads', but it was surrendered when the nearby town of Devizes fell to Oliver Cromwell in 1645. John Ivory-Talbot inherited the abbey and made substantial alterations in the 1750s, with a Gothic-inspired entrance arch, oriel windows and the Great Hall.

The scientist and inventor William Henry Fox Talbot lived his entire life at Lacock Abbey (1800–77), where he set his mind to solving the problem of 'fixing' an image (since he felt his paintings and drawings were not good enough). In due course, he captured an image of a latticed oriel window at Lacock in 1835, now celebrated as the first-ever surviving photographic

negative. His daughter called his small wooden cameras ‘little mousetraps’.

The estate was given to the National Trust by Matilda Talbot in 1944, and the Fox Talbot Museum opened in 1975. Visitors can see one of Fox Talbot’s mousetrap cameras and learn about the birth and science of photography.

Feature films shot at Lacock Abbey include *Moll Flanders* (1996), *Harry Potter and the Philosopher’s Stone* (2001), *Harry Potter and the Chamber of Secrets* (2002), *The Other Boleyn Girl* (2008), *Harry Potter and the Half-Blood Prince* (2009) and *Fantastic Beasts: The Crimes of Grindelwald* (2018). Television series include *Pride and Prejudice* (1995), *Cranford* (2007) and *Downton Abbey* (2015).

Below: *Sheep still graze in the grounds of Lacock Abbey.*

Right: *The simple box camera Fox Talbot constructed in 1830 with a photograph made from the earliest camera negative seen behind it.*

Longleat House

Built in the 16th century, Longleat House is situated near the towns of Warminster in Wiltshire and Frome in Somerset, and combines an immaculate Elizabethan prodigy house with 1,000 acres of parkland designed by Lancelot 'Capability' Brown, as well as a safari park containing over 500 animals. Longleat has always been owned by the Thynn dynasty; the original house was purchased in 1541 for £53 by John Thynn (who worked in Henry VIII's kitchens), but was destroyed by fire in 1567 and then rebuilt. Thynn's descendants still live there today – an incredible 15 generations on – and it is the seat of the Marquess of Bath.

The name comes from the English *leat*, an artificial waterway supplying water to a watermill, and the house's first function was as an Augustinian priory. John Thynn's vast number of descendants made many improvements to the estate.

In the late 17th century, James Thynn commissioned Christopher Wren to make some modifications. A new front door, hall and staircase were built, and a family tree dating back to 1215 now stands at the foot of the staircase.

Thomas Thynn, 1st Viscount of Weymouth (1640–1714), began collecting rare books and started

The form of Longleat's frontage dates from the 16th century and it remains beautifully symmetrical.

the house's first library (there ended up being seven libraries containing 40,000 books). He was inspired by the formal gardens at the Palace of Versailles in Paris, and commissioned George London to create decorative parterres, canals, fountains, paths, avenues and terraced flower beds. Christopher Wren added the Best Gallery, Long Gallery, Old Library and Chapel.

The 2nd Viscount of Weymouth (1710–51) married Louisa Carteret, and her ghost, known as the 'Green Lady', is said to haunt the house. The 1st Marquess of Bath (1734–96) commissioned 'Capability' Brown to transform the formal gardens into a landscaped park, and the 2nd Marquess (1765–1837) had the house modernized, and

replaced Wren's staircase with a Grand Staircase in the Gothic Revival style.

Longleat House was used as a hospital during World War I, and then became a school in World War II. In order to raise funds, Henry Thynn, 6th Marquess of Bath, opened the house to the public in 1949, making it the first-ever English stately home to be run as a commercial enterprise. A safari park was added in 1966 – the first drive-through safari park outside Africa. In 1975, several elaborate and challenging mazes were constructed using yew trees. The Hedge Maze is the largest and most difficult of these to navigate, with swirling curves, dead ends, bridges and a central tower.

The estate was formerly the location of a long-running *Doctor Who* exhibition, and the documentary series *Animal Park* (2000–present) is filmed there. As well as being open to the public, it remains a private residence for Ceawlin Thynn, Marquess of Bath, and his wife Emma.

Above: *The 90ft-long Saloon houses this massive Carrara marble fireplace, copied from the Doge's Palace in Venice.*

Left: *Four members of a pride of lions, two females and two young males relax on their specially built platform.*

Montacute House

A late Elizabethan mansion set in Montacute in South Somerset, Montacute House is a supreme example of well-preserved English Renaissance architecture. It is a large and noble prodigy house that has remained virtually unchanged since it was built in

1598, and it has been used as a location for many costume dramas and literary adaptations.

Built from glowing honey-coloured Ham Hill stone and featuring a Long Gallery illuminated by a continuous wall of glass, the house was commissioned by the English lawyer and politician Sir Edward Phelips, whose family had lived in the area since 1460. Phelips

Below and inset: *Montacute House and its grounds seen from the air with a detail of one of the summerhouses.*

went on to become Speaker of the House, Master of the Rolls and prosecutor during the Gunpowder Plot trial of 1605. He hired the mason William Arnold to build the three-storey house to showcase his wealth, ambition and showmanship. The Long Gallery is the longest of its kind in England, and contains a collection of 60 Tudor and Elizabethan portraits on loan from the National Portrait Gallery in London.

Subsequent generations of Phelips' descendants lived at Montacute House until the beginning of the 20th century. In 1915, it was let to George Curzon, 1st Marquess Curzon of Kedleston, who lived there with his mistress, the British romantic novelist Elinor Glyn. In 1923, it was let to the

wealthy New York writer Henry Lane Eno, who had inherited a fortune from his family's real estate and banking businesses. He died there in 1928. The next owner was the philanthropist Ernest Cook, who presented the house to the Society for the Protection of Ancient Buildings, and from there, to the National Trust. Montacute House and its surrounding gardens opened to the public in 1932, but it was temporarily requisitioned by the army in World War II for billeting US soldiers prior to the D-Day landings in Normandy (1944).

Notable features of the E-shaped house include the Great Hall, kitchens and pantries, the Library (formerly known as the Great Chamber, where Phelips entertained his guests with music and dance), the Crimson Chamber and the Hall Chamber, a dining room containing a delicately worked 500-year-old tapestry, and the Long Gallery, where glass windows span the entire length of the top floor. The walled gardens, pavilions and courtyards were originally created in 1633, and were replanted and maintained by Ellen Phelips from 1840 until her death in 1911.

Above: *The window of the Great Chamber depicts the arms of families connected to the Phelips by marriage.*

Left: *The detail of the Great Chamber, the strapwork ceiling, bookcases and grand fireplace, dates from the 19th century.*

Montacute House has appeared in films such as *Sense and Sensibility* (1995), *The Hound of the Baskervilles* (2000), *The Libertine* (2004) and *Wolf Hall* (2015), and it was the inspiration for Tottington Hall in *Wallace & Gromit: The Curse of the Were-Rabbit* (2005).

Tyntesfield

Near Wraxall (close to Bristol) in North Somerset, Tyntesfield is a spectacular Victorian Gothic Revival estate that was designed not as an ostentatious statement of wealth, but simply as a family home. It is richly decorated with ornate Gothic carvings and surrounded by kitchen gardens, terraces, lakes and woodlands.

The name comes from the Tynte baronets who owned land in the area in the 1500s, and the

Left: *Tyntesfield is a superb example of a Victorian country house library.*

Right: *The house has many elements of Gothic Revival style.*

house was originally a hunting lodge. In the late 1700s, Tyntes Place was owned by Sir John Tynte and was approached by an avenue of elm trees, but when he moved away it was leased out and downgraded to a farmhouse. A Georgian mansion was built on the site in the 1830s, and William Gibbs, who had made his fortune from importing and marketing Peruvian guano for use as a fertilizer, purchased the property in 1843. He renamed it Tyntesfield and set to work rebuilding and expanding the mansion, most notably adding a chapel in the 1870s.

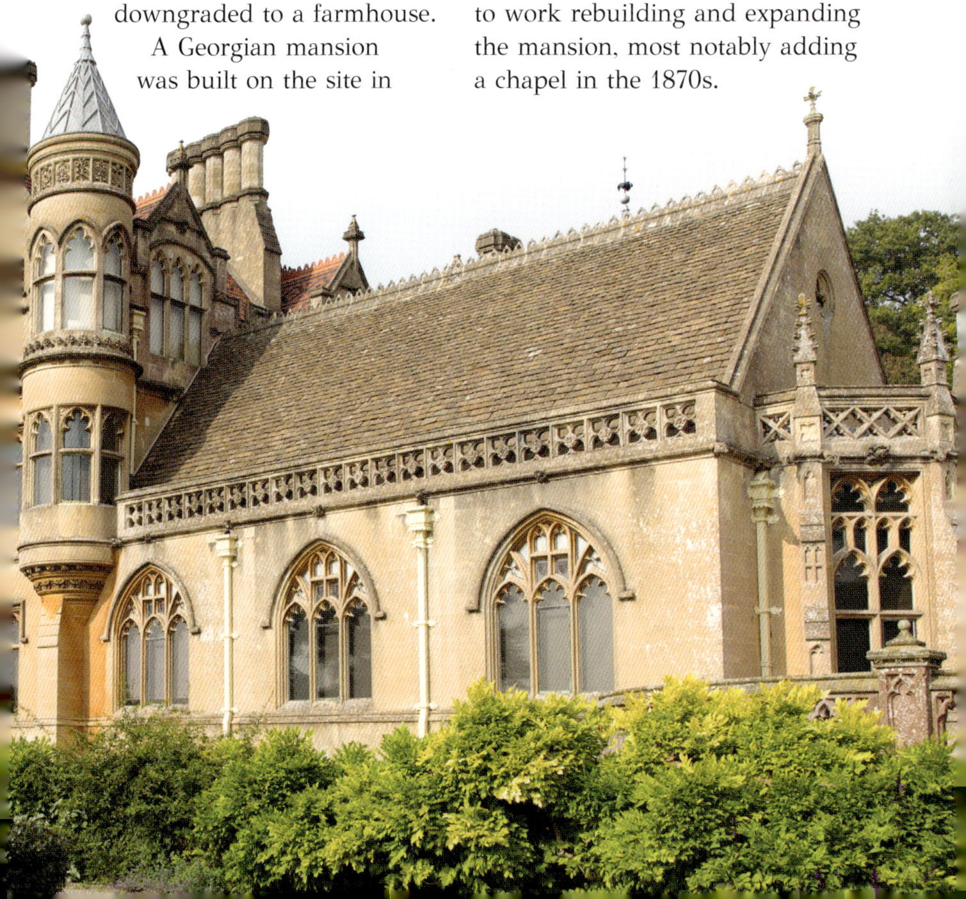

Above: *The kitchen garden has provided fruit and vegetables since the 1860s.*

Right: *Packed with high Gothic features, the chapel was added by William Gibbs.*

The house remained in the Gibbs family until 2001, at which point it was purchased by the National Trust.

Tyntesfield is a very pretty house built using two different types of Bath stone: one ochre and the other reddish. It contains spiralling turrets, an elaborate roof with asymmetrical pitches and gables, an enormous conservatory and a Gothic chapel inspired by Sainte-Chapelle in Paris. Stunningly decorated, the chapel features exquisite stained-glass windows, a colourful mosaic floor, flowering brass chandeliers and beautiful stonework.

The house is brimming with more than 60,000 treasures, including silverware, books and artworks. One of the most famous paintings is a 17th-century portrait, *Saint Lawrence holding his Gridiron and crowned by a Putto-angel* by Spanish artist Zambrano of St Lawrence, which hangs in the middle of one of the hall walls.

The estate includes a kitchen garden, a rare surviving example of a late Victorian orangery, an aviary for exotic birds (converted into a playhouse) and a sawmill, all surrounded by 150 acres of wooded parkland. The area is an important habitat for bats, including the threatened lesser horseshoe bat and greater horseshoe bat; maintenance and repairs are scheduled to avoid the bats' breeding seasons.

Tyntesfield has been used as a location for television dramas such as *Doctor Who* ('Hide', 2013) and *Sherlock* ('The Abominable Bride', 2016), and as a film set for Agatha Christie's *Crooked House* (2017).

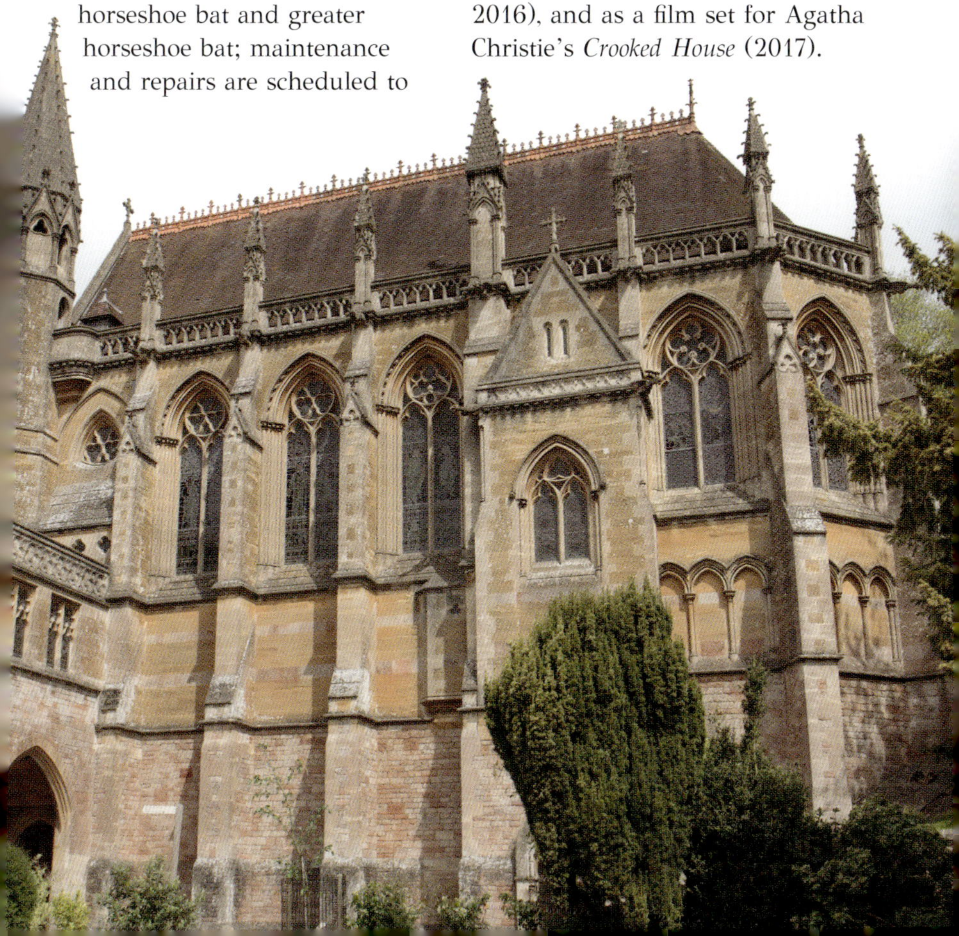

Saltram

Left: *The Saloon at Saltram was the subject of a major restoration project in 2017–18.*

Right: *Saltram's creamy façade, one of the best preserved examples of an early Georgian house.*

Overlooking the River Plym near Plymouth in Devon, Saltram is a hidden treasure set among rolling woodland landscape. The house is one of Britain's best-preserved Georgian mansions, its contents giving a fascinating insight into well-to-do 18th-century country life. The architectural historian Sir Nikolaus Pevsner described it as 'the most impressive country house in Devon'.

The Saltram estate originally belonged to George Parker in 1712, and was passed down through three generations of the Parker family. George's son John began making improvements in 1743, and his son (also called John; later Lord Boringdon) hired the Scottish architect Robert Adam to alter the Tudor building further, expanding and improving it significantly. The Saloon (drawing room) in particular is considered to be one of Adam's finest neoclassical interiors, with its huge plasterwork ceiling, delicate Chinese wallpaper, gilded furnishings and dramatic crystal chandeliers.

Other highlights include an exceptional collection of paintings – many by Sir Joshua Reynolds and Angelica Kauffmann – a superb library and a garden complete with an 18th-century orangery, several follies, beautiful shrubberies and trees, and a chapel (now a tea room).

In its heyday, Saltram included 4,000 acres of land and employed many local workers, and the park is still a working estate today. It includes farmland, beaches, saltmarshes, meadows, woodland, an estuary and an amphitheatre.

Saltram has a literary link to Jane Austen in that Frances, the third John Parker's second wife, corresponded with her in the early 1800s. Cementing this link, the house appeared as the home of the Dashwoods in the film *Sense and Sensibility* (1995).

CHAPTER 3

ENGLAND
East

England's eastern half has some of the grandest – and quirkiest – houses of all. Near Saffron Waldon in Essex is Audley End House, remarkable perhaps more for its contents – an astonishing array of taxidermy – than the house itself. Another unique house is Ickworth in Suffolk with its unmistakeable Palladian rotunda. Hatfield House in Hertfordshire is the model of an early Jacobean mansion with beautiful formal gardens, Burghley in Cambridgeshire is a wonderfully ornate example of a Tudor palace, with its many spires and turrets. Woburn Abbey retains little of its ecclesiastical past, but was rebuilt as a beautiful house in the Palladian style during the 18th century. And near the coast in Norfolk is the immense Holkham Hall showing its dramatic scale on every level.

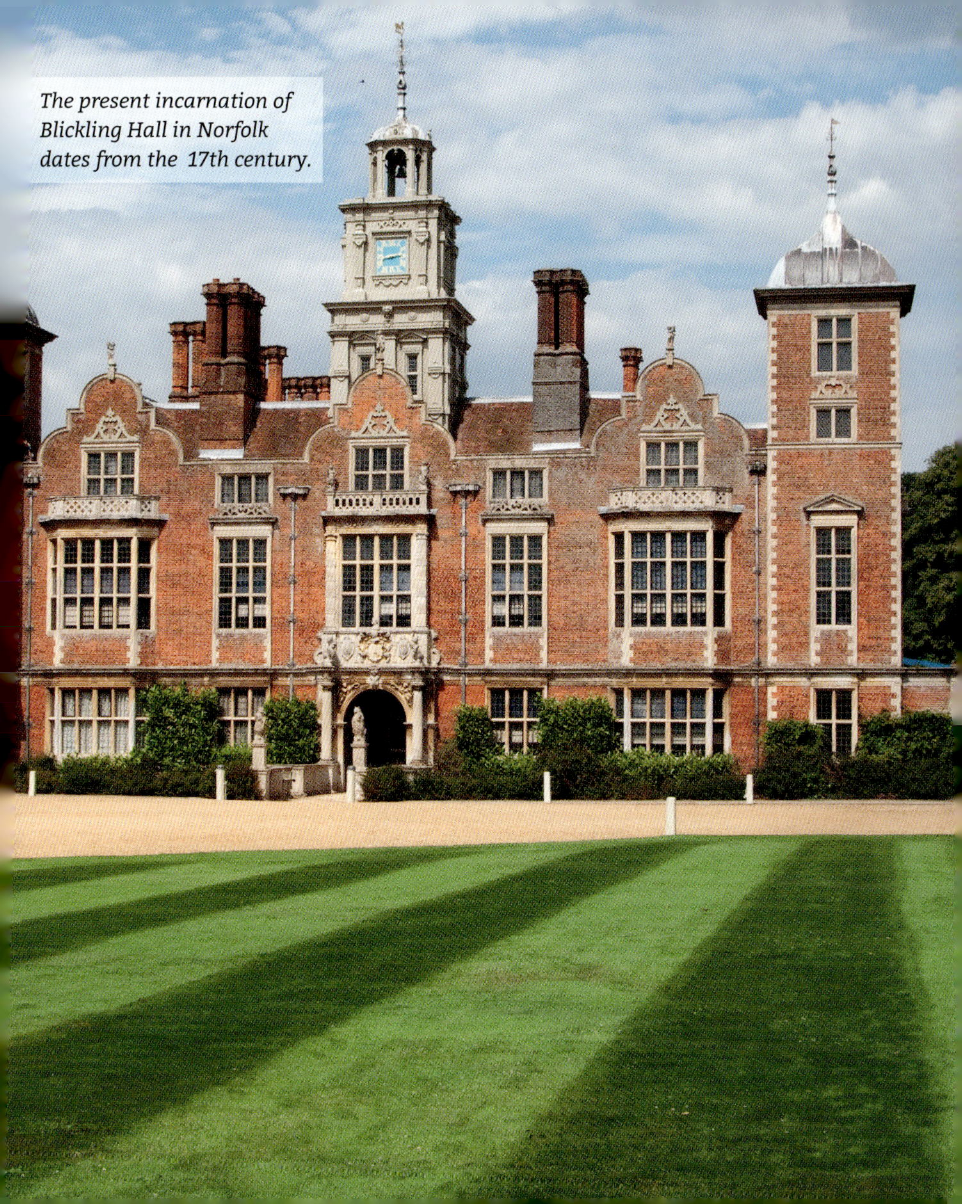

The present incarnation of Blickling Hall in Norfolk dates from the 17th century.

Audley End House

Situated just outside the town of Saffron Walden in Essex, Audley End House is one of Britain's finest examples of 17th-century Jacobean architecture. It was designed as an opulent prodigy house fit for royalty, and although it is now only a third of its original size, conservation work has restored it to its former glory.

Walden Abbey was founded on the site in 1190, but in 1538 during the Dissolution of the Monasteries, Henry VIII granted the building to Sir Thomas Audley, Lord Chancellor, who transformed it into a domestic mansion. It was subsequently rebuilt by Audley's grandson Thomas Howard, 1st Earl of Suffolk, in the early 1600s, at which point it became the largest private residence of its day. Elizabethan in style, it included a magnificent façade featuring turrets, pinnacles, parapets and large windows, and two porches for the king and queen.

The house was leased by Charles II in 1666, and then returned to the Howard family in 1701. Elizabeth, Countess of Portsmouth, bought the property in 1751 and saved it from decay. Many changes were made: the architect Sir John Vanbrugh demolished most of the forecourt and constructed a Baroque screen to the main staircase; Robert Adam designed new reception rooms and refurbished the south wing in the classical 18th-century style; and Lancelot 'Capability' Brown landscaped the grounds.

Richard Neville, 3rd Baron Braybrooke, inherited Audley End House in 1825 and restored many of its Jacobean features, such as the Great Hall's ornate oak screen and the Grand Chamber's dolphin and sea monster plasterwork (hence its alternative name, the Fish Room). Richard Griffin, 4th Baron

Braybrooke, built up an extensive collection of paintings, furniture and taxidermy.

During World War II, Polish soldiers of the Special Operations Executive trained at Audley End House for parachuting into German-occupied Poland. The house remained in the possession of the Barons Braybrooke until the 9th Baron sold it in 1948 to

The 4th Baron's extraordinary collection of taxidermy, primarily birds, is housed in glass cases throughout the house.

the Ministry of Works (which later became English Heritage).

The Adam Suite was fully restored in the 1960s, and the house today is an excellent restoration of Adam's designs, with neoclassical rooms featuring jewel-like adornments on the walls and ceilings, furniture commissioned especially for royal visits and paintings by Canaletto, Jan Asselijn, Jan Brueghel the Younger and Giovanni Battista Cipriani.

The house has been used in television shows such as *Antiques*

Roadshow (2016) and *Gardeners' Question Time* (2017), and appeared in the Netflix series *The Crown* (2019).

The back of the house with its glorious colourful summer gardens, awash with vibrantly hued planting.

Luton Hoo

Near Luton in Bedfordshire and Harpenden in Hertfordshire, Luton Hoo has been through several transformations: a family home, burnt-out ruin, magnificent palace and most recently a luxury five-star hotel. The house played an important role in World War II and has been home to a Prime Minister and a member of the Russian Imperial family, and has appeared in many films.

The Saxon word *Hoo* means the spur of a hill, and the estate dates back to 1601 when it was

bought by Robert Napier. A succession of different houses were built on the site, with today's mansion being designed by the neoclassical architect Robert Adam in 1767 for John Stuart, 3rd Earl of Bute and Prime Minister to George III. Lancelot 'Capability' Brown remodelled the gardens

Main image: *Luton Hoo's classical frontage still bears the stamp of the great Robert Adam despite later remodelling.*

Below: *Borne aloft by mermen, the fountain torrent comes through a putti cradling a fish atop a large shell.*

The extensive formal gardens at the back of the house are part of a larger scheme for the grounds by 'Capability' Brown.

and parklands, and created two naturalistic lakes by damming the River Lea.

In 1830, John Crichton-Stuart, 2nd Marquess of Bute, employed the architect Sir Robert Smirke (who had recently designed the British Museum) to redesign the house with a grand portico at the entrance, sympathetic to Robert Adam's earlier designs. A fire destroyed much of the house and its contents in 1843, and five years later it was sold to a Liverpool solicitor, John Shaw Leigh, who restored it.

Luton Hoo remained in the Leigh family until 1903, when it was bought by the diamond magnate Sir Julius Wernher. Using his personal fortune, Wernher commissioned Charles Mewès and Arthur Davis (who had designed London's Ritz Hotel) to create opulent Edwardian Belle Époque interiors to show off his many treasures. Highlights included a fabulous curved marble staircase adorned with Giulio Bergonzoli's statue *The Love of Angels*, and a stunning blue Great Hall filled with valuable tapestries, Louis XV furniture and Sèvres porcelain.

In 1917, Wernher's son Harold married 'Lady Zia', a member of the former Russian Imperial family, and Luton Hoo's already impressive collection was enhanced further with works by the jeweller Peter Carl Fabergé (many eggs of which were stolen in 1994).

Luton Hoo was used as Headquarters for the Eastern Command during World War II. Military tanks were tested on the estate during the war, and Sir Winston Churchill addressed a crowd of 110,000 people after the war to thank them for their support. Queen Elizabeth and Prince Philip spent part of their honeymoon at Luton Hoo in 1947.

The house passed to Sir Harold and Lady Zia's grandson Nicholas Phillips in 1977, and when he died in 1991, the estate was sold and the art collection moved to Ranger's House in Greenwich, London. Luton Hoo was subsequently bought by Elite Hotels and 1999, and the newly named Luton Hoo Hotel, Golf and Spa opened in 2007, offering 228 elegant bedrooms, fine cuisine, a championship golf course and luxury spa set amid 1,000 acres of landscaped parkland.

Luton Hoo has been used extensively in films, including *Never Say Never Again* (1983), *The Secret Garden* (1993), *Four Weddings and a Funeral* (1994), *Mrs Brown* (1997), *Wilde* (1997), *Eyes Wide Shut* (1999), *The World is Not Enough* (1999), *Sexy Beast* (2000), *Quills* (2000), *Enigma* (2001), *Little Dorrit* (2008), *War Horse* (2011), *The World's End* (2013) and *Mr Turner* (2014).

Hatfield House

Located in Hatfield, Hertfordshire, Hatfield House is the current home of Robert Gascoyne-Cecil, 7th Marquess of Salisbury. It was built in 1611 by Robert Cecil, first Earl of Salisbury and chief minister to James I, and has remained in the Cecil family for generations. It is a superb example of a Jacobean prodigy house, filled with historic mementos collected over 400 years.

Henry VIII's children – including the future Elizabeth I – spent their youths at the Royal Palace of Hatfield, which was a short distance away from the present house. Some of the palace has been preserved, and visitors today can see many of Elizabeth's possessions and historical documents, including her gloves and stockings, her famous *Rainbow Portrait* (one of the most colourful Tudor portraits in existence), as well as the Queen Elizabeth Oak

Hatfield House's superb Jacobean features look out onto a meticulously planned formal garden.

Left: *Named for James I, this elegant salon contains a statue of the king which stands above the mantelpiece.*

Right: *The East Garden next to the house is formally planted with a topiary, parterre, herbaceous borders and vegetable garden.*

in the grounds. Legend has it that Elizabeth was sitting under the tree when she learnt of Mary I's death, and hence her succession to the throne of England.

Following Elizabeth I's reign, James I gave the palace to his chief minister Robert Cecil, who demolished most of it in 1608 and used the bricks to build the current Hatfield House. He kept certain Jacobean features, such as the elaborately carved wooden Grand Staircase and the chapel's stunning stained-glass window featuring scenes from the Old Testament. His descendant Robert Gascoyne-Cecil, 3rd Marquess of Salisbury and Prime Minister during Queen Victoria's reign, entertained important guests at Hatfield House with enormous banquets, dances and masques. The phrase 'Bob's your uncle' is said to refer to him.

Interior highlights include the lavishly decorated Marble Hall with a chequered black and white floor; the King James Drawing Room with beautiful tapestries, portraits and a life-size statue of James I; the Library housing over 10,000 volumes dating back to the 16th century; the marble-floored Armoury with a Dutch organ still used for concerts today; and the Victorian Kitchen where a team of 25 staff produced feasts for Victoria and her guests.

The park and gardens are vast in scale, and include a magnificent water sculpture designed by contemporary sculptor Angela Conner, as well as orchards, terraces, fountains, herb gardens, a maze and a deer park.

Films shot at Hatfield House include *Greystoke: The Legend of Tarzan, Lord of the Apes* (1984), *Batman* (1989), *Batman Returns* (1992), *Orlando* (1992), *Shakespeare in Love* (1998), *Sleepy Hollow* (1999), *Lara Croft: Tomb Raider* (2001), *The Importance of Being Earnest* (2002), *Lara Croft Tomb Raider: The Cradle of Life* (2003), *Elizabeth: The Golden Age* (2007), *Sherlock Holmes* (2009) and *The Favourite* (2018). Television series include *Band of Brothers* (2001) and *Antiques Roadshow* (2010).

Woburn Abbey

Situated in the village of Woburn in Bedfordshire, Woburn Abbey has been the family seat of the Duke of Bedford since the mid-1500s, and is currently home to the 15th Duke, Andrew Russell. The house and gardens are open to the public for part of the year, and the art collection is among the finest in private hands. The outdoor landscape features a deer park, miniature railway and safari park.

Woburn Abbey was originally a Cistercian monastery, but after its dissolution by Henry VIII in 1538, Edward VI gave it to Sir John Russell, who became 1st Earl of Bedford in 1550. Russell demolished the original abbey and built a new house, but kept the name 'Abbey'.

From 1744 onwards, Henry Flitcroft rebuilt the West Wing for the 4th Duke of Bedford, turning Woburn Abbey into a

Woburn Abbey's ecclesiastical origins have been largely erased by 18th-century remodelling which has given the house its Palladian styling.

graceful Palladian house with a Grand Staircase, elaborate State Apartments and outdoor Stable Blocks. Henry Holland, added a Library and Book Room filled with botanical and ornithological volumes, including *Birds of America* by John James Audubon.

In 1817, the world's first ecological experiments were done in the Abbey Gardens and influenced Charles Darwin in his theory of the origin of species. In the 1840s, Duchess Anna Maria Russell, wife of the 7th Duke and lifelong friend of Queen Victoria, popularized the ritual of afternoon tea by providing tea and cakes or sandwiches for her guests. Famous visitors included John Adams (the future second President of the United States) and Thomas Jefferson (the future third President), as well as Queen Victoria and Prince Albert.

Woburn Abbey was used as a military hospital in World War I. In World War II, Woburn Abbey was used as a propaganda headquarters and residence for Wrens from Bletchley Park. It was opened to the public in 1955, and from 2000–14 the gardens were restored to their original 1787 designs, including the reconstruction of a Chinese Dairy for displaying porcelain, dishes and plates.

Wrest Park

As well as being a magnificent 1830s stately home located in Silsoe in Bedfordshire, Wrest Park is also renowned for its glorious grounds that bring to life the history of the English garden. There are charming follies, garden buildings and statues, a Wellingtonia tree dating from 1856 (one of Britain's earliest examples of a Christmas tree), and 92 acres of 18th-century landscape designed by Lancelot 'Capability' Brown.

From the 1400s, the Wrest estate belonged to a leading aristocratic family, the de Greys. Successive generations developed the enormous formal woodland garden, and in 1710 Thomas Archer designed

a fine French-influenced Baroque pavilion with *trompe l'oeil* wall paintings and a dome topped by a golden orb finial. Around 1758, 'Capability' Brown added a canal and woodland, creating picturesque vistas along the many pathways.

Built in 1834–9, the present house was designed by Thomas de Grey, 2nd Earl de Grey, who adopted the 18th-century French style of architecture, creating something of a French château. Opulently decorated rooms include the Grand Staircase, Library, Drawing Room and Dining Room, and the old kitchen garden was replaced with a vast walled garden. The house was used as a convalescent home during World War I, but fell into decline after a fire in 1916. It became a centre for agricultural engineering research in 1948, and was taken over by English Heritage in 2006. A memorial column dedicated to 'Capability' Brown can be seen in the gardens, and an ambitious 20-year project to restore the gardens, fountains and monuments to their pre-1917 state was put into action in 2008.

Above: *Thomas Archer's pavilion, built 1709–1711, has magnificent trompe l'œil paintings by Mark Anthony Hauduroy.*

Left: *The back of the house looking out onto the gardens shows the detail in its roofline.*

Burghley House

A spectacular 16th-century Tudor palace, Burghley House is located in Cambridgeshire near Stamford. The rooms, furnishings and grounds provide an accurate glimpse into the lifestyle of the aristocracy during the time of Elizabeth I, earning it the reputation as 'England's greatest Elizabethan house'.

Burghley House was built between 1558 and 1587 for Sir William Cecil (later 1st Baron Burghley), Elizabeth I's chief advisor and Lord High Treasurer, following the style of Richmond Palace. It remained in the Cecil family – the Earls of Exeter – for generations until being taken over by a preservation trust set up by Lord Burghley's descendants. It has been extremely well preserved for over 450 years.

The main part of the house has 35 major rooms on the ground and first floors, and there are

more than 80 smaller rooms, halls, corridors, bathrooms and service areas. The stonemasonry is a fine example of Elizabethan architecture and proportion; the floorplan was originally in the shape of the letter 'E' (in honour of Elizabeth), but the north-west wing was later demolished to allow better views of the parkland designed by the famous landscape architect Lancelot 'Capability' Brown.

The State Rooms have been preserved exactly as they were in the 17th and 18th centuries, including a collection of several hundred paintings acquired by John Cecil, 5th Earl of Exeter, and Brownlow Cecil, 9th Earl, both of whom made multiple trips to Italy and brought back artworks by the Old Masters. There are also fine collections of Oriental and European ceramics, English and Continental furniture, 17th-century antiques and a unique collection of Chinese snuff bottles. Decorative highlights include ceiling paintings by Antonio Verrio (in the Heaven Room and George Rooms), wall paintings by Thomas Stothard (above the Hell Staircase) and ceiling and wall paintings by Louis Laguerre (in the Bow Room).

Above: *Burghley's 18 state rooms are packed with paintings and grand furniture.*
Left: *The limestone used to build Burghley is so durable that on the south front many blocks retain the masons' identifying marks.*

The unaltered Elizabethan façade of Burghley House makes it ideal for use in period dramas including films such as *Pride and Prejudice* (2005), and *Elizabeth: The Golden Age* (2007), and television series such as *Middlemarch* (1994), *The Curious House Guest* (2005) and *Bleak House* (2005).

Ickworth House

Above: *The library at Ickworth has one of the National Trust's finest collections.*

Right: *Ickworth's iconic rotunda is at the heart of the house and dominates the beautiful gardens.*

Located near Bury St Edmunds in the rolling countryside of Suffolk, Ickworth House is an Italianate palace with formal gardens, pleasure grounds and an ancient deer park.

The house was built between 1795 and 1829 to entertain guests and showcase the valuable treasures of the Hervey family, later Marquesses of Bristol. The flamboyant Frederick Hervey, 4th Earl of Bristol, known as the Earl Bishop, commissioned the Italian architect Antonio Asprucci – who had worked on the Villa Borghese in Rome – to design a classical villa to display his magnificent art collection. The collection, however, was confiscated by Napoleonic troops in 1798, and English architects Francis and Joseph Sandys adapted the plans and finished the work after the Earl Bishop had died (1803).

Frederick's son, also named Frederick, became the 5th Earl of Bristol (later 1st Marquess of Bristol), and turned the East Wing galleries into a family home and the central Rotunda into a gallery.

The West Wing was left empty and used for storage.

The impressive art collection includes paintings by Titian, Nicolas Poussin, Diego Velázquez, William Hogarth, Joshua Reynolds, Thomas Gainsborough, Angelica Kauffmann and Élisabeth Vigée Le Brun, and the focal point of the entrance hall is John Flaxman's immense 18th-century marble sculpture *The Fury of Athamas*, depicting a Greek tragedy of madness and murder. The house also contains one of the National Trust's largest collections of silver, as well as *objets de virtu*, fans, books and Regency furniture and porcelain.

Blickling Hall

From the Old English meaning 'homestead of Blicla's people', Blickling Hall is part of the Blickling Estate in Blickling, Norfolk. A great 17th-century Jacobean mansion, it was mentioned in the Domesday Book and was the birthplace of Anne Boleyn. The grand red-brick house contains one of the most historically significant collections of manuscripts and books in England, and is set within formal and informal gardens surrounded by two deer parks.

The styling of Blickling in its current form has much in common with Hatfield House, also designed by Robert Lyminge.

The original house was the property of Thomas and Elizabeth Boleyn, whose three children Mary, Anne and George were born there in the early 1500s. In 1616, the Boleyn house and estate were purchased by Sir Henry Hobart, who asked Robert Lyminge (architect of Hatfield House) to replace the Tudor house with the current red-brick building.

Hobart's son John inherited the estate in 1626 and became 1st Earl of Buckinghamshire. He converted the Long Gallery into a Library filled with books from the scholar Sir Richard Ellys. John also added a ha-ha (a sunken fence that preserved the view of the landscape) and a Doric Temple.

The estate passed to Lady Caroline Hobart (later Lady Suffield) in 1793. During her long tenure, the gardens were developed by Humphrey Repton and his son John Adey Repton. Caroline also commissioned Joseph Bonomi to design an pyramidal Mausoleum as a memorial to her father.

Caroline had no children, so the estate devolved to her nephew William Kerr, 8th Marquess of Lothian, and it thereafter remained in the Kerr family. Famously, Philip Kerr, 11th Marquess, persuaded Prime Minister Winston Churchill to write a letter to President Franklin Roosevelt informing him of Britain's depleted military strength and appealing for US aid during World War II. The estate passed into the care of the National Trust in 1940, and aircrew from nearby RAF Oulton were billeted at Blickling Hall during the war.

Houghton Hall

Located in the parish of Houghton in Norfolk, Houghton Hall was commissioned in 1722 by Britain's first Prime Minister Sir Robert Walpole, 1st Earl of Orford. It is one of the finest Palladian houses in Britain, designed specifically to display the wealth, taste, power and status of its owner. Just a stone's throw from Sandringham House, Houghton Hall was constructed using fine-grained, silver-white stone with large domes at each corner, and the interior rooms are brightly coloured and opulent. The surrounding parkland, consisting of 'twisting wilderness paths' with ha-ha barriers (sunken fences), was designed in the 18th century by Charles Bridgeman.

Walpole used two eminent architects of the day, Colen Campbell and James Gibbs, to design the exterior structure, while William Kent decorated the lavish interiors. The house became something of a museum due to Walpole's passion for art. He amassed a fabulous collection of over 400 paintings by artists such as Rubens, van Dyck, Velázquez, Rembrandt and Poussin – arguably the greatest collection of European art in Britain.

The house was passed down to Walpole's son and then grandson, 3rd Earl of Orford, who sold the picture collection to pay off debts. In 1797, the 3rd Earl's sister, Lady Mary, Countess of Cholmondeley, inherited the house, and it has remained with the Cholmondeleys ever

since. As the family's ancestral seat was at Cholmondeley Castle in Cheshire, Houghton Hall remained untouched and unchanged for over a century, only being periodically inhabited for shooting parties. It was restored to its former glory just after World War I by George Cholmondeley, 5th Marquess of Cholmondeley, and his wife Sybil.

Houghton Hall is currently the residence of David Cholmondeley, 7th Marquess of Cholmondeley, with certain parts open to the public. Highlights include the sumptuously decorated State Rooms, an incredible collection of 20,000 model soldiers in the Stable Block, a 5-acre walled garden, a 13th-century church and herds of white fallow deer.

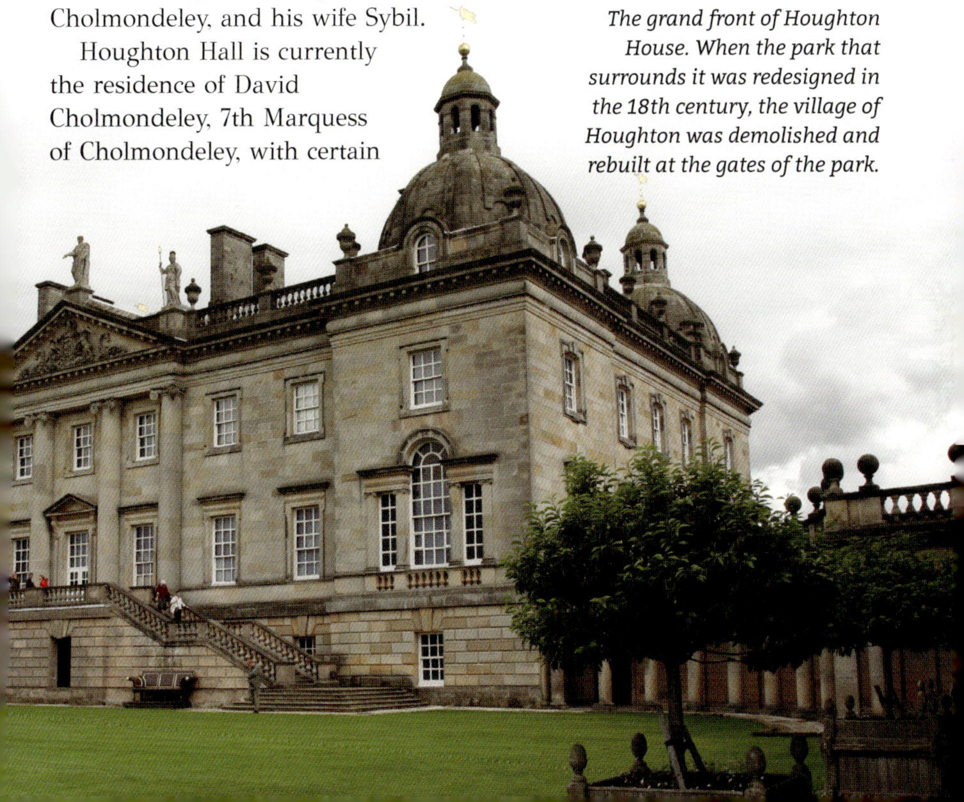

The grand front of Houghton House. When the park that surrounds it was redesigned in the 18th century, the village of Houghton was demolished and rebuilt at the gates of the park.

Holkham Hall

Adjacent to the village of Holkham on the wind-swept north Norfolk coast, Holkham Hall is a beautifully preserved 18th-century Palladian house, with one of the most outstanding collection of paintings and sculptures of any stately home. There are works by Rubens, van Dyck, Poussin and Gainsborough, as well as ancient Roman marble sculptures.

The Holkham Estate was originally purchased in 1609 by Sir Edward Coke (pronounced 'Cook'), and Holkham Hall was built between 1734 and 1764 by his son Thomas Coke, 1st Earl of Leicester. Thomas had spent six years touring Europe, and during his time abroad he collected many great works of art and literature.

In Rome, he met the architect Lord Burlington and his protégé William Kent, well known for their enthusiasm for the Palladian Revival style. Together, they developed the concept for Holkham Hall: a Palladian-style mansion filled with valuable art, sculpture and books. The house had a yellow-brick exterior and was influenced by the construction of nearby Houghton Hall.

Thomas died in 1759 without seeing his project completed, but

Left: *Holkham is built on a truly grand scale, both in terms of its Palladian architecture and the great grounds that encompass the house.*

Below: *On a smaller scale, a gateway in a walled garden.*

his widow Lady Margaret Tufton carried on the works for the next 17 years, the inside of the house becoming known as the finest Palladian interior in England. The estate passed briefly to Thomas's nephew Wenman Roberts, who took the name of Coke, and from him to his son Thomas William Coke (later 1st Earl of Leicester of Holkham). Thomas William was a politician and agriculturalist with great energy and charm, and was popularly known as 'Coke of Norfolk'. He worked as a Member of Parliament for 53 years.

The epic Marble Hall (actually made of softer, more translucent

alabaster rather than marble) serves as a spectacular entrance to the house, set over two levels with a 50-foot gilded plaster dome ceiling and beautifully carved pink Derbyshire alabaster pillars. The smooth, white staircase leads to the State Rooms on the *piano nobile* (first floor), the most majestic of these being the Saloon with walls lined with crimson velvet and adorned with paintings by Rubens and van Dyck.

Other notable rooms include the Green State Bedroom and North State Sitting Room, both decorated with large 17th-century tapestries; the Landscape Room, with 22 works by Old Masters, including seven by the great French landscape painter Claude Lorrain; and the Old Kitchen, once bustling with 60 servants producing 1,700 meals per month. The Statue Gallery is believed to contain the most complete collection of classical statuary in any private house in Britain, with Roman works dating from the 1st to the 3rd centuries AD. There are also three libraries

on the first floor: the Manuscript Library, once the principal bedroom; the Classical Library, once the ante room to Coke of Norfolk's bedroom and later a collection of early printed books; and the Long Library, used by the family for entertaining.

Holkham Hall remains the family home of the Earls of Leicester of Holkham. With its rich history, well preserved architecture and situation on a 25,000-acre estate on the Norfolk coast, it is a prime location for film sets. It has appeared in *Shakespeare in Love* (1998), *All the King's Men* (1999), *The Lost Prince* (2003), *The Duchess* (2008), *Dean Spanley* (2008), *Glorious 39* (2009) and *Annihilation* (2018).

Above: *Holkham's Marble Hall is clad in Derbyshire pink alabaster and its domed ceiling rises 50ft high.*

Left: *The Saloon at Holkham Hall, hung with many fine paintings.*

Sandringham House

Privately owned by Queen Elizabeth II and probably best known as the country home where the Windsors spend their Christmases, Sandringham House stands within a 20,000-acre estate near Sandringham in Norfolk. More than 200 staff are employed in the grounds, including gamekeepers, gardeners and farmers, with a great emphasis on recycling and conservation. The Queen gave her first televised Christmas message from Sandringham in 1957.

Originally recorded as 'Sant Dersingham' in the Domesday Book of 1086, the name was later shortened to Sandringham. A large manor was built on the site at

the time of Elizabeth I, and then replaced with a Georgian mansion in 1771.

In 1862, the estate was purchased for Queen Victoria's eldest son Albert Edward, Prince of Wales (later Edward VII) as a country home for him and his fiancée Princess Alexandra of Denmark. Soon after their marriage, Albert and Alexandra needed more space for their growing family, so they demolished the house and built a new one in 1870 (designed by Robert William Edis), later adding a ballroom and a guest accommodation wing in the 1890s.

When Edward VII died in 1910, Sandringham House passed to his son George V. George's affection for the place was evident when he wrote: 'Dear old Sandringham, the place I love better than anywhere else in the world', and in the first-ever Christmas message (written by Rudyard Kipling) in 1932, he said: 'I speak now from my home and from my heart to you all.'

Left: *The Queen's Norfolk country estate's current house dates from the 1870s.*

Below: *One of the salons at Sandringham shown in a photograph taken for a women's magazine c.1910.*

The estate was inherited by Edward VIII in January 1936. He was unhappy there, however, and when he abdicated in December of that year, the house and grounds were purchased by his brother George VI. Like his father, George adored Sandringham; he wrote to his mother Queen Mary: 'I have always been so happy here and I love the place.' His life was cut short, though, and when he died in 1952, the house passed to his daughter, Elizabeth II. The Queen has followed the tradition of her royal ancestors, spending two months of every winter at Sandringham. It was opened to the public in 1977 for her Silver Jubilee.

Built with red brick, limestone dressings and Norfolk carrstone, the house is Jacobean in style, similar to the nearby Blickling Hall. The largest room is the

Left: *York Cottage, built as an overflow for the main house was much loved by George V who furnished it himself.*

Right: *One of the gatehouses at Sandringham. Some other gatehouses are now available as holiday rentals.*

Saloon, once used as a venue for dancing but now a reception room adorned with portraits of Queen Victoria and Prince Albert. The stunning Drawing Room has white and gold walls, white marble statues and a patterned red carpet, and is where members of the royal family gather before official occasions. The oak-panelled Dining Room is painted in light green and decorated with wall-to-wall murals and Spanish tapestries, including some by Goya. The Ballroom was added by Edis in 1884 as an alternative to the Saloon for entertaining, and the Queen now uses it for high tea, entertainments and as a cinema.

Sandringham House remains almost exactly as it was in Edwardian times. Visitors can see portraits, *objets d'art*, porcelain and silver, as well as an important collection of Oriental and Indian arms and armour that was collected by Edward VII on his tour of the East in 1875–6.

CHAPTER 4

ENGLAND
East Midlands

England's east central counties hold some of its most iconic houses. Chatsworth House in Derbyshire near Bakewell is renowned for the splendour of the house, the interiors and its setting, enhanced by 'Capability' Brown in the 18th century. Hardwick Hall (right), the home of Bess of Hardwick, is perhaps the classic example of a grand Elizabethan house. Kirby Hall in Northamptonshire, though partially ruined, retains its grace and beautiful grounds. Belvoir Castle in Leicestershire benefits from its hilltop location, the reason a medieval castle was once built on the site. Newstead Abbey still has many of the ecclesiastical features, including windows and cloisters from its former existence as a religious building.

The Elizabethan architecture of Hardwick Hall, as viewed from the walled garden.

Kirby Hall

Known as one of the greatest Elizabethan and 17th-century houses in England, Kirby Hall is located near Gretton in the district of Corby, Northamptonshire. It was once owned by Sir Christopher Hatton, Lord Chancellor to Elizabeth I, and is a prime example of a prodigy house.

The original medieval house and estate were purchased by Sir Humphrey Stafford in 1542. His son, also called Humphrey, remodelled it because he needed a home to reflect his rising social status – he became Sheriff of Northamptonshire in 1566 and Elizabeth I had stayed in the area. In 1570, construction began on Kirby Hall in a quasi-French style with classical Greek and Roman elements, the idea being to create a grand rectangular layout with an inner courtyard.

In 1575, the property was purchased by one of Elizabeth I's courtiers, Sir Christopher Hatton of Holdenby, who added a suite of formal rooms for royal visitors. The house then passed through various relations until it came to Sir Christopher Hatton III, and the famous architect Inigo Jones was brought in to transform the outmoded Elizabethan house into a grand Jacobean mansion, with a symmetrical design and formal gardens. In 1670, the estate passed

Kirby Hall's scale and grandeur is still apparent despite it's current state, with the far half of the building being roofless.

to Hatton III's son, Sir Christopher Hatton IV, Governor of Guernsey. Being a keen plantsman, he remodelled the gardens further, creating the stone-edged 'cutwork' Great Garden punctuated by statues, urns, seating and topiary. Remaining in the Kirby family until 1764, Kirby Hall next passed to the Finch-Hattons, the descendants of whom still own the estate today.

The present house is in a semi-ruined state and partly roofless, but the Great Hall and State Apartments are intact and have been refitted and sumptuously decorated in the authentic 17th- and 18th-century style.

Kirby Hall has appeared in films such as *Mansfield Park* (1999), *A Christmas Carol* (1999) and *Tristram Shandy: A Cock and Bull Story* (2005), and television series such as *Civilisation* (1969) and *Antiques Roadshow* (2014).

Belvoir Castle

Once the site of an 11th-century Norman castle, Belvoir Castle is a stately home on top of a high hill in Leicestershire, overlooking the Vale of Belvoir. The name, pronounced 'Beaver', means 'beautiful view' in French, and on a clear day it is possible to see Lincoln Cathedral 30 miles away. The house has been in the Manners family since the 1500s, and the seat of the Duke of Rutland since the 1700s.

By 1464, the first timber castle was left in ruins because of the War of the Roses, and a second castle was built in 1555 by Sir Thomas Manners, 1st Earl of Rutland. Manners used stone to create a much nobler structure with a central courtyard, some of which remains today.

The second castle was destroyed during the Civil War of 1642–51, and a third castle was designed for John Manners, 8th Earl of Rutland, by John Webb, a pupil of the English classical architect Inigo Jones. The building was remodelled as a palatial country house rather than a castle, and by the time of the 9th Earl (1st Duke of Rutland), the famous landscape designer Lancelot 'Capability' Brown was brought in to add lakes and woods.

'Capability' Brown's plans were never carried out, however, and John Manners, 5th Duke of Rutland, and his wife Elizabeth oversaw a fourth incarnation from 1801–32. James Wyatt, the Gothic Revival architect who had recently made improvements at Windsor Castle, was asked to do the designs, and this is the version we see today. Under the enthusiastic eye of Elizabeth, Belvoir was transformed from a run-down structure into a fairy-tale dream home, one of the finest examples of Regency architecture in Britain.

In 2014, the abandoned plans of 'Capability' Brown – missing since a fire in 1816 – were rediscovered, and a two-year project was instigated by Emma Manners, 11th Duchess of Rutland, to bring his 'lost landscape' to life. The restored Pleasure Gardens were opened in 2016 to coincide with the 300th anniversary of 'Capability' Brown's birth in 1716.

As a film location, Belvoir Castle has appeared in films such as *Young Sherlock Holmes* (1985), *The Haunting* (1999), *The Da Vinci Code* (2006), *The Young Victoria* (2009), *A Royal Night Out* (2015) and *Victoria and Abdul* (2017), and the Netflix series *The Crown* (2017).

Belvoir Castle sits proudly atop its thickly forested slopes.

Newstead Abbey

Best known as the ancestral home of Lord Byron, Newstead Abbey is situated between Nottingham and Mansfield in Nottinghamshire. It was originally an Augustinian priory in 1163–73, then converted into a domestic stately home after Henry VIII's Dissolution of the Monasteries.

A series of Byrons owned the house, the first being Sir John Byron of Colwick in 1540. The fourth laid out the gardens and ponds in the early 1700s, and the fifth, known as the Wicked Lord, built two castellated forts and some Gothic follies, but neglected the house and stripped the woodland of its trees to raise money. His great-nephew, the famous poet George Gordon Byron (later known simply as Lord Byron) became the 6th Baron Byron and inherited the property in 1798, aged 10.

Lord Byron lived at Newstead Abbey between 1808 and 1814, and he carried out major decorative renovations. His beloved Newfoundland dog, Boatswain, is buried on the grounds, and Byron's *Epitaph to a Dog* inscribed on the animal's gravestone is one of his most famous works:

Near this Spot
are deposited the Remains of one
who possessed Beauty without Vanity,
Strength without Insolence,
Courage without Ferosity,
and all the virtues of Man without his Vices.
This praise, which would be unmeaning Flattery
If inscribed over human Ashes,
is but a just tribute to the Memory of
BOATSWAIN, a DOG,
who was born in Newfoundland *May 1803*
and died at Newstead *Nov. 18th 1808.*

Newstead Abbey still has much that recalls its most famous inhabitant, including the desk where Byron wrote much of his finest poetry.

Byron wanted to be buried with his dog, but debts forced him to sell. Colonel Thomas Wildman became the next owner in 1815, and he restored and expanded the estate. The African explorer William Frederick Webb was the next owner, carrying out further building and gardening works, but largely preserved the existing house. Webb's grandson Sir Julian Cahn presented the estate to the City of Nottingham in 1931.

Visitors can see Lord Byron's portraits, manuscripts and furniture, as well as exploring the walled and Japanese gardens set among beautiful lakes and streams.

Chatsworth House

Situated on the River Derwent between Bakewell and Chesterfield in Derbyshire, Chatsworth House has been passed down through 16 generations of the Cavendish family since 1549. The name comes from *Chetel's-worth*, meaning 'the Court of Chetel': during the reign of Edward the Confessor, a Norseman named Chetel owned the land, but he was deposed after the Norman Conquest.

Sir William Cavendish, Treasurer of the King's Chamber, acquired the estate in 1549, and his wife Bess began building the house in 1553. After Cavendish died, Bess finished the house and lived there with her fourth husband George Talbot, 6th Earl of Shrewsbury.

Right: *The extraordinary Painted Hall at Chatsworth with its ceiling showing scenes from the life of Julius Caesar.*

Below: *Chatsworth House in its matchless setting in the Peak District as painted by William Marlow.*

From 1570, Shrewsbury was charged with the custody of Mary, Queen of Scots, and her stays there earned the top floor room facing the inner courtyard the name 'the Queen of Scots room'. When Bess died in 1608, her eldest son Henry inherited Chatsworth, then his brother William Cavendish, 1st Earl of Devonshire, purchased it for £10,000. It has remained in the Cavendish family ever since.

During the mid-18th century, the 4th Duke of Devonshire made some changes to the estate, altering the approach so that it was from the west and commissioning Lancelot 'Capability' Brown to redesign the gardens. Brown's new arrangement gave the 1st Duke's original formal gardens a more naturalistic appearance and style.

In the early 1800s, the 6th Duke undertook a major transformation of the house and gardens over an extensive 47-year period. He was an avid collector, especially of sculpture and books, and either built or repurposed entire rooms to show off his possessions. In 1830, he turned his attention to a series of guest bedrooms for his party guests, decorating them with hand-painted Chinese wallpapers and fabrics.

Above: *The Dining Room, part of the 6th Duke's renovation, is used for fomal dinners.*

Right: *Holding one of the most significant collections of books still in private hands, the Library at Chatsworth has two levels.*

Following a series of financial problems for the Devonshire family starting in the 1950s, the house, its contents and assorted land were acquired by the trustees of the Chatsworth Settlement, later the Chatsworth House Trust, with the intention of maintaining the house for the benefit of the public. The 11th Duke's widow, the Dowager Duchess of Devonshire, made many improvements to the gardens, creating a kitchen garden, cottage garden and a maze, and adding contemporary sculptures. In 2008, a ten-year programme of improvement works was initiated at a cost of £32 million. Stonework, statues, paintings, tapestries and water features were all renovated – the most extensive restoration that had been made in 200 years.

The house has 126 rooms; the majority are closed to visitors so that the family are able to live privately, but the rest are accessible to the public. The lavish State Apartments, featuring the Great Chamber (originally reserved for royalty), are decorated with ceiling paintings and murals, and the public can also view the magnificent Painted Hall, Sketch Galleries and a Sculpture Gallery.

Works on display include ancient Roman and Egyptian sculpture, and masterpieces by Rembrandt, Joshua Reynolds, Paolo Veronese, Lucian Freud, Edmund de Waal and David Nash.

The grounds cover more than 100 acres, requiring a staff of 20 full-time gardeners. Notable features include the Cascade (a set of stone steps over which water flows from fountains at the top), Canal Pond, Emperor Fountain, Willow Tree Fountain, Rockery, the 1st Duke's Greenhouse, and also the beautiful Rose, Cottage and Kitchen Gardens. A farmyard provides close encounters with ponies, lambs and pygmy goats, and in 2018 the Trout Stream was replanted, having been the inspiration for the Best Show Garden at the 2015 RHS Chelsea Flower Show. Beyond the gardens, the estate includes a further 1,000 acres of parkland, woods and farmland.

Chatsworth House has been the site for many television and film shoots over the years, including Mr Darcy's home in *Pride and Prejudice* (2005), *The Duchess* (2008), *The Wolfman* (2009), *Death Comes to Pemberley* (2013), *Peaky Blinders* (2014) and *The Crown* (2016).

Above: The Rape of the Sabines *dominates the Painted Antechamber at Chatsworth.*

Left: *The grand entrance to the house still belies its actual scale, and has superb vistas over the exquisite grounds.*

Hardwick Hall

Designed by Robert Smythson in 1590–99, Hardwick Hall is an Elizabethan country house sitting atop a hill between Chesterfield and Mansfield in Derbyshire. One of the earliest examples of the Italian Renaissance style of architecture (which spread from Florence to England), it was built for the Countess of Shrewsbury, Elizabeth Talbot (née Hardwick), a shrewd businesswoman who became known as 'Bess of Hardwick'.

Born on the site of the old hall, Bess married four times, rising to a high level of nobility in English society and becoming immensely powerful and wealthy in the process. Indeed, she was described

Left: *The dining room at Hardwick is on a relatively modest scale, with its formal wood panelling and arrangement of portraits.*

Right: *Hardwick Hall is the archetype of a splendid Elizabethan house, with its Renaissance influences and great scale.*

as the second most important woman in England after Queen Elizabeth I. Before Hardwick, she already owned Chatsworth House (her second husband was Sir William Cavendish).

Living mostly at Hardwick, Bess oversaw substantial architectural changes over the years. She began by making improvements to the old house, and then progressed to constructing a second, even more grand house a few yards away. The new hall proved to be an extraordinary achievement, rivalling any other grand house of the Elizabethan age, and provided Bess with a lavish home for her family.

As well as being one of the finest Elizabethan houses in England, Hardwick Hall is also an excellent example of a 'prodigy house' – a large, ostentatious English country house built with the aim of housing Elizabeth I on royal visits. The rectangular, turreted building exemplified contemporary ideals of symmetry and used enormous

grids of glass, giving rise to a local rhyme: 'Hardwick Hall, more glass than wall.' Each of the towers is adorned with the initials 'E.S.' for Elizabeth Shrewsbury, with the countess's coronet mounted above.

The interior consists of three main storeys, each with a higher ceiling than the level below. The elaborately decorated rooms feature spectacular coloured plasterwork, friezes and fireplace overmantels, together with Flemish tapestries, Elizabethan embroideries, Persian table-carpets, painted wall-hangings, inlaid furniture, beautiful ceramics and other decorative objects, scores of

Left: *The High Great Chamber with its superb frieze depicting hunting scenes and travels to exotic lands.*

Right: *The Long Gallery runs the whole length of the east side of the house.*

historical portraits and the finest collection of 16th- and early 17th-century needlework in the world – much of which was catalogued in 1601 by Bess herself.

Outdoors, there are four courtyards divided by sandstone walls, each with their own individual character: the North Court was originally an orchard and was later converted into a carpark, but there are plans to restore it; the West Court contains herbaceous borders, the lawns of which were originally designed in the shape of Bess's 'E.S.' monogram; the East Court is a lawn with a small pond in the middle; and the South Court is subdivided into four squares containing vegetables, orchard fruits, herbs and a nuttery.

Bess's descendants worked conscientiously to ensure the preservation of Hardwick Hall through to 1959, when the Dukes of Devonshire transferred ownership to the National Trust. It is a Grade I listed building that is open to the public, and it has been used in films such as *Harry Potter and the Deathly Hallows: Part 1* (as the exterior for Malfoy Manor, 2010) and *Mary Queen of Scots* (2018).

CHAPTER 5

ENGLAND
West Midlands

The counties of the West Midlands are sometimes thought of as the functional centre of England's industrial heart, but many beauty spots and gracious homes belie this narrow view. Baddesley Clinton, dating from the 16th century, is a delightful moated manor house in the heart of England. At Stoneleigh Abbey, just to the east of Coventry, the ruins of the former abbey can still be seen next to the 17th-century house with later additions. Hanbury Hall in Worcestershire is a red-brick mansion in the Queen Anne style, while Attingham Park in Shropshire is an elegant Georgian house with an early 19th-century picture gallery designed by the great architect, John Nash.

Stoneleigh Abbey lies on the banks of the River Avon. The steps in the foreground run down to the water's edge.

Baddesley Clinton

Situated within its own parkland near Warwick in Warwickshire, the moated manor house of Baddesley Clinton began life as a simple forest clearing, and later served as a sanctuary for hiding persecuted Catholics. It has been in the Ferrers family since 1517.

The estate is named after a medieval Saxon farmer called Baeddi who cleared a space for grazing in the Forest of Arden, and the de Clinton family who subsequently dug the moat in the 13th century. In 1438, the site was bought by a wealthy lawyer, John Brome, who built much of the present house using locally quarried stone. It passed to his son and then granddaughter, who

Left: *The main entrance to Baddesley Clinton is via a bridge across the small moat.*

Right: *Built on a modest scale, the interiors at Baddesley Clinton are cosy and homely rather than grand although with some beautiful carvings and tapestries.*

married Sir Edward Ferrers, Sheriff of Warwickshire.

Edward's grandson Henry Ferrers, known as 'the Antiquary', lived at Baddesley Clinton from 1564 to 1633, and made many improvements. He rebuilt the Great Hall in brick and decorated the stained-glass windows and wood carvings with the family's coat of arms. In 1590, he rented the house to two Catholics – the Vaux sisters – who built three priest holes under the kitchen, and from then on, Baddesley Clinton became a hiding place for Jesuit priests.

The house was refurbished in the 1860s while inhabited by four friends known as 'the Quartet': Baddesley's heir Marmion Ferrers and his artist wife Rebecca Orpen, and Rebecca's aunt, the novelist Lady Georgina Chatterton and her second husband Edward Dering. The four spent their time at Baddesley Clinton reading, writing and painting, while also restoring the house and rebuilding the Catholic Chapel.

Open to the public since 1982, visitors can see the Great Hall, Drawing Room, Chapel and Library, as well as Henry Ferrers' bedroom. The extensive formal gardens feature peaceful fishponds, a walled garden and a lake, along with several 18th-century farm buildings.

Stoneleigh Abbey

With humble beginnings in 1154 as a Cistercian monastery, Stoneleigh Abbey became a family home after the Dissolution of the Monasteries in 1538, and is now best known for its connection to the novelist Jane Austen. The ancestral seat of the Leigh family, it has also played host to royalty such as Charles I and Queen Victoria.

Some of the original 14th-century abbey can still be seen today, most notably the red-brick Gatehouse. In 1558, the estate was sold to the Lord Mayor of London, Sir Thomas Leigh, and remained in his family from 1561 until 1990.

The house has two halves: the 17th-century red sandstone Jacobean house built from the monastery ruins and a silver-stone West Wing designed in the 18th century by Francis Smith of Warwick in Baroque style. In 1809, Rev. Thomas Leigh commissioned Sir Humphry Repton to

update the grounds, and he created a stunning natural landscape, a cricket pitch and bowling green.

Thomas's cousin Cassandra Austen had two daughters, the watercolorist Cassandra and the novelist Jane. Both sisters stayed at Stoneleigh in the early 1800s, and the fictional town of Sotherton Court in Jane Austen's *Mansfield Park* (1814) was inspired by Stoneleigh Abbey. Austen described the interior rooms, the food, the servants and the views of the grounds in detail, and even included the real-life landscape gardener Humphry Repton in the story.

The most impressive room in the West Wing is the ornately decorated Saloon, where Queen Victoria and Prince Albert dined in 1858, and the interiors and furniture are much as they were in Jane Austen's time. The Orangery is now a tea room with a magnificent view over Repton's landscape and the River Avon, and the gardens contain the thousand-year-old 'Shakespeare Oak', one of the oldest trees in Britain.

Left: *Francis Smith's West Wing overshadows the original Jacobean house at Stoneleigh.*

Right: *A grand room for receiving royalty and other VIPs, the Saloon retains much of its late 18th-century style.*

Hanbury Hall

An 18th-century house in Worcestershire, Hanbury Hall has been the seat of the Vernon family for 300 years. A two-storey red-brick house in the Queen Anne style, it is surrounded by 400 acres of gardens and parkland.

The estate's first Vernon was Rev. Richard Vernon (1549–1628), and the present house was built c.1706 for his descendant, Thomas Vernon a lawyer. He commissioned Sir James Thornhill, who had worked on the Dome of St Peter's Cathedral, the Painted Hall at Greenwich and the Great Hall of Blenheim Palace, to create wall and ceiling paintings. His murals depicting Greek myths can still be seen today. The formal gardens were designed by George London, and included a parterre, fruit garden and wilderness.

Thomas bequeathed Hanbury Hall to his cousin Bowater Vernon, who spent the family fortune, and from him it went to Emma Vernon, who married Henry Cecil, the 1st

Marquess of Exeter, in 1776. Emma and Henry remodelled parts of the house and replaced the formal gardens with English landscapes in the style of 'Capability' Brown. Emma married three times, and it is said that her ghost, dressed in black, lingers on the grounds.

A few generations of Vernons later, Hanbury Hall passed to Sir Bowater George Vernon, 2nd Baronet of Hanbury, in 1920. He became estranged from his wife, adopted his 15-year-old parlour maid Ruth and began expressing far-right political views. Poor health and a belief that arrest was imminent led him to shoot himself in his bedroom in 1940. He left his fortune to Ruth and gave Hanbury Hall to the National Trust.

Above: *Early planting in the garden parterres in the designs originally set out by George London.*

Left: *The red-brick Queen Anne style frontage of Hanbury Hall.*

Since then, the garden parterres have been faithfully restored to George London's original designs, and visitors can view an orangery, ice house, two domed gazebos, orchards, a walled garden and a mushroom house.

Attingham Park

With spectacular views across 200-year-old parkland, Attingham Park is a classically designed stately home set in a Humphry Repton landscape near Atcham in Shropshire. It was built in 1785 for the first Lord Berwick, and has a chequered history of rising and falling fortunes.

Receiving his title in 1784, Noel Hill, 1st Baron Berwick, commissioned the architect George Steuart to replace an older building on the site with a grander country house to go with his new status. In 1805, a Picture Gallery was added by architect, John Nash, who went on to work on Buckingham Palace, the Theatre Royal in London and the Royal Pavilion in Brighton. The ceiling had curved glass panels set within a cast iron frame to provide natural light.

Noel's son Thomas inherited Attingham Park when he was 19 and became the 2nd Lord Berwick. After he married in 1812, he and his wife Sophie began running through the family fortune to the point of bankruptcy, and they auctioned almost all the family paintings and furniture and moved to live in Italy.

Left: *Attingham Park's kitchen with its substantial collection of brass pots and other historic kitchen implements.*

Right: *The classical frontage of the house with its pillared entrance.*

Thomas's younger brother William became the 3rd Lord Berwick and tried to buy back as much of the contents of the house as possible. He managed to acquire a collection of 18th-century Italian furniture, some from Caroline Murat, Napoleon's sister.

Circumstances changed again when Richard, 4th Lord Berwick, drank too much and allowed the house to fall into ruin. He did produce enough sons to keep Attingham Park in the family for several more generations. Another Richard, 5th Lord Berwick, established a famous herd of Hereford cattle, commemorated in oil paintings of the prized animals.

The last family member to live at Attingham Park was Thomas, 8th Lord Berwick, and he and his wife Teresa (daughter of the painter Thomas Hulton) became its saviours. They restored the house and filled it with paintings, sculpture, furnishings and carpets. Charles Noel-Hill, 9th Lord Berwick, gave the estate to the National Trust.

As well as appreciating the house as one of the most complete Georgian houses to be found in Britain, visitors to Attingham Park can also explore the stable block, toll house, red-brick walled garden, bee house, ice house and ha-ha (sunken fence).

CHAPTER 6

ENGLAND
North East

Home of the Yorkshire Dales and Moors and the dramatic coastlines of Northumberland, the north east of England also has a number of exceptional stately homes. Wentworth Woodhouse in South Yorkshire, is renowned for the great length of its frontage. Castle Howard, mainly designed by John Vanbrugh in the Baroque style, is comparable in scale to the great palaces of Europe and took more than 100 years to build. Norton Conyers in North Yorkshire is more humble, a late medieval house that was added to in the 17th century but retains a modest scale. Harewood House, almost its neighbour, is splendid, a beautifully kept Georgian mansion with extensive grounds and a superb collection of art. Finally, Northumberland is home to the innovative Cragside with its dramatic setting and host of technological advances that were amazing for its time.

Harewood House, near Harrogate in North Yorkshire, as seen from the terrace.

Wentworth Woodhouse

Highly recognizable from its immense façade, Wentworth Woodhouse is located in the village of Wentworth in Rotherham, South Yorkshire. The façade is actually the longest of any English country house – at 606 feet long, it is more than twice the length of Buckingham Palace. It is the largest private home in Britain, and is set within 180 acres of gardens and grounds, with magnificent views over parkland and lakes. The stables can accommodate 100 horses and are so big that visitors sometimes stop there, mistaking them for the house.

Both the house and the village of Wentworth are associated with three aristocratic families:

the Wentworths, Watsons and Fitzwilliams.

In the 1630s, the original house was built for the ill-fated Thomas Wentworth, 1st Earl of Stafford and advisor to Charles I. Wentworth tried to strengthen the king's position against Parliament, and for this he was condemned to death and executed in 1641. Thomas's son William inherited the house, but upon his death the property was unexpectedly bequeathed to William's cousin Thomas Watson (instead of his son Thomas Wentworth), thus setting in motion several generations of arguing and competition. Fortuitously, this rivalry led to improvements being made to Wentworth Woodhouse and the nearby Stainborough Hall (also known as Wentworth Castle), each owned by competing branches of the family.

By the 1720s, Thomas Watson-Wentworth, 1st Marquess of Rockingham, had rebuilt the house

The extraordinary length of Wentworth Woodhouse's frontage is apparent from this perspective view.

A pretty wisteria-draped summerhouse within the grounds of Wentworth Woodhouse.

in the red-brick English Baroque style, then his son Charles, 2nd Marquess and later Prime Minister, added many follies. These included the Needle's Eye, a 46-foot pyramid with a narrow archway through the bottom, said to have been designed so that a coach and horses could 'pass through the eye of a needle'.

Throughout the 18th century, Wentworth Woodhouse was expanded and improved by architects such as Inigo Jones, Ralph Tunnicliffe, Henry Flitcroft and John Carr. Its social reputation was cemented by welcoming guests such as the American statesman Benjamin Franklin and members of the Royal family. When the Prince of Wales and the Duke of York arrived, reams of visitors came to get a glimpse, and the house became a symbol of grandeur as well as a leading centre of Whig politics.

The third family, the Fitzwilliams (related by marriage),

took over ownership in 1782 and remained there until the late 20th century. First, they made alterations to the landscape: the rough ground was remodelled into more pleasing shapes, a serpentine pool was constructed and many trees were planted. Next, the discovery of coal on the land raised enormous amounts of money, elevating the Fitzwilliams to one of the wealthiest families in England.

In its heyday, Wentworth Woodhouse contained more than 300 exquisitely furnished rooms and employed about 1,000 staff working as butlers, housekeepers, maids, cooks, carpenters, gardeners, stablehands and gamekeepers. The young Princess Victoria stayed there in 1835, and George V and Queen Mary visited in 1912 (the latter being the inspiration for the plotline of the 2019 film *Downton Abbey*). By the time of the 6th Earl's death in 1902, the Fitzwilliam fortune was said to be the equivalent of £3 billion today.

After World War II, however, events took a turn for the worse. The country's demand for coal soared after the war, and the government ordered opencast mines to be dug out on the estate. Much of the house's valuable art and furniture was sold, and as well as ruining the gardens and making it difficult for the family to live there, the digging work caused structural damage to the house's foundations. In 1948, Peter Wentworth-Fitzwilliam, 8th Earl of Fitzwilliam, died in a plane crash with his lover Kathleen Kennedy (sister of the future US President John F. Kennedy), and left no male heir.

The house passed to a second cousin who had no children, was then sold to Wensley Grosvenor Haydon-Baillie, an unsuccessful English businessman who did a limited amount of restoration, and then sold again in 1999 to a London architect Clifford Newbold for the mere sum of around £1.5 million. Newbold converted parts of the house into a museum, but he died in 2015 before the work was completed. The house went

on the market again, but this time it was sold to the Wentworth Woodhouse Preservation Trust for £7 million.

Plans are currently afoot for restoring the house to its former glory while keeping it open to the public. The British government has awarded £7.6 million to repair the damage caused by the post-war mining operations, and the National Trust has also agreed to help fund the restoration project. Since 2019, much of the building has been covered in scaffolding, and repairs are expected to take many years.

Events that regularly take place at Wentworth Woodhouse include concerts, classic car shows, author talks, weddings, film screenings, garden parties and craft markets. The house has featured in television period dramas such as *Jonathan Strange & Mr Norrell* (2015) and *Victoria* (2016), and feature films such as *Darkest Hour* (2017).

Wentworth Woodhouse gardens have Italianate-style gardens and a great maze to explore.

Castle Howard

Castle Howard's Atlas fountain, with its sculpture of Atlas bearing the world on his shoulders, was turned on in 1853 as part of the improvements by the 7th Earl of Carlisle.

The famous setting for *Brideshead Revisited*, Castle Howard is a private stately home in North Yorkshire, and one of the great palaces of Europe. It has been the home of the Howard family, the Earls of Carlisle, since 1699.

The site chosen for the house was the ruined Henderskelfe Castle, which had been built during the reign of Edward III by the Greystoke family. Charles Howard, 3rd Earl of Carlisle, asked his friend John Vanbrugh to help him create a flamboyant Baroque-style mansion, despite Vanbrugh never having done anything like it before. Vanbrugh famously went on to design Blenheim Palace, but did not live to see the finished result at Castle Howard, because construction took more than 100 years, lasting from 1699 until 1811.

The house today is not the symmetrical design that Vanbrugh envisaged, but a combination of an elaborate Baroque East Wing and a more conservative Palladian West Wing, the latter designed by the 3rd Earl's son-in-law, Sir Thomas Robinson.

The Chapel is part of the West Wing and was originally planned as a dining room, but in the 1870s the floor was lowered and the room redecorated in the pre-Raphaelite style. It features brightly coloured wallpapers, rugs designed by William Morris and stained-glass windows by Edward Burne-Jones.

In 1940, a fire destroyed about a third of the house, including the Great Hall, Dining Room, eastern State Rooms and the Dome, which collapsed into the Great Hall. The ceiling painting *The Fall of Phaeton* by Antonio Pellegrini was lost, along with two Tintorettos and several valuable mirrors.

A few years after being opened to the public in 1952, the house was lovingly restored and the Dome rebuilt and redecorated under the direction of the 9th (and final) Earl of Carlisle, George Howard. It is one of the largest country houses in England, with a total of 145 rooms.

The gardens are also extensive, covering 1,000 acres and featuring magnificent vistas across the Howardian Hills. An 18th-century walled garden near the house contains heritage roses, vegetables and formal parterres, and beyond that there are beautiful lakes, terraces, fountains, woodlands, follies, temples and statues. The Atlas Fountain (1850), with four Greek gods blowing jets of water over a large bronze globe held aloft by Atlas, is one of the most photographed features in the grounds.

In 1981, Castle Howard was immortalized in the public eye in the form of the enormously successful television adaptation of Evelyn Waugh's 1945 novel *Brideshead Revisited* (starring Jeremy Irons). The house served as the titular home of the wealthy aristocratic Marchmain family, visited by Sebastian Flyte's Oxford friend, Charles Ryder. The 2008 film version (starring Matthew Goode) was also filmed there. Other dramas shot at Castle Howard include the film *Garfield: A Tale of Two Kitties* (2006), as well as the TV series *Death Comes to Pemberley* (2013) and *Victoria* (2016).

Above: *Lined with classical statuary, the Antique Passage runs for much of the length of the house.*

Left: *Vivid decoration and fine furniture in the Turquoise Drawing Room.*

Norton Conyers

A late medieval manor house with Stuart and Georgian additions, Norton Conyers is located about four miles north of Ripon in North Yorkshire. The novelist Charlotte Brontë visited in 1839, and was told the legend of a mad woman being confined to the attic. This, along with the house's blocked staircase connecting the first floor to the attic, is said to have given Brontë the idea for Mr Rochester's insane wife in her novel *Jane Eyre* (1847).

The estate dates back to the Domesday Book, when it was owned by the Bishop of Durham.

In 1398, it was sold to Sir Richard Norton, Chief Justice of England, and from then on passed through several generations of Nortons. Another Richard took part in an unsuccessful attempt to replace Elizabeth I with Mary, Queen of Scots, and was accused of high treason in 1569.

In 1624, Norton Conyers was acquired by the English politician and Royalist army soldier Sir Richard Graham, and the estate has remained in the Graham family ever since. Notable visitors included Charles I (1633) and James II (1679), who stayed there when travelling to Scotland. The royal bedroom and the bed they slept on are on display today.

The two-storey house is timber-framed with Dutch-style gables, a four-bay frontage and a Westmorland slate roof, and the interior features 18th-century plaster ceilings, fine furniture, costumes and ceramics. There is a collection of family portraits in the Great Hall and on the main staircase, and also a picture of horses entitled *The Quorn Hunt* (1822) by the celebrated British artist John Ferneley.

The large walled garden near the house dates from around 1760, and has English-style plantings of flowers, fruit and vegetables around a central orangery. There are also clipped yew hedges, colourful herbaceous borders and an ornamental pond.

The many gabled exterior of Norton Conyers, a house with style echoes from several eras.

Harewood House

Just north of Leeds in West Yorkshire, Harewood House is the opulent home of the Lascelles family, and one of the ten Treasure Houses of England. A historic Georgian property with a magnificent art collection, extensive gardens, a lake, bird garden and animal farm, it is also the film location of the drama *Emmerdale*.

The house was built from 1759 until 1771 for Edwin Lascelles, 1st Baron Harewood. Edwin's father, Henry, made his fortune from the West Indian sugar trade. Edwin hired the best professionals in the

country to create his grand estate: the Yorkshire architect John Carr designed the building; Robert Adam decorated the rooms; Thomas Chippendale provided the furniture; and 'Capability' Brown designed the 1,000-acre parklands.

In the 1840s, Henry Lascelles, 3rd Earl of Harewood, commissioned Sir Charles Barry – who was simultaneously working on the Palace of Westminster – to enlarge the house. Barry added an Italianate balustrade to the front, additional storeys above each of the wings, and a Terrace Garden in the grounds.

Harewood House remains in the Lascelles family, and after a period as a convalescent hospital during World War II, it was opened to the public in 1970. Visitors can see an exquisite collection of Renaissance masterpieces, portraits by Sir Joshua Reynolds, Thomas Gainsborough, John Hoppner and Sir Thomas Lawrence, landscapes by J.M.W. Turner, modern artworks collected by the 7th Earl of Harewood, and a fine collection of Sèvres china. The grounds include a Walled Garden, a Lakeside Garden, a Himalayan Garden, a Bird Garden with over 40 species of exotic birds, and opportunities to meet alpacas, pygmy goats and pot-bellied pigs.

The house has appeared in films such as *King Ralph* (1991) and *Downton Abbey* (2019), and dramas such as *Emmerdale* (1996), *Death Comes to Pemberley* (2013) and *Victoria* (2016).

Harewood House has many good sides, including the rear view over the meticulously planned formal gardens.

Cragside

Dramatically cut into a steep, rocky valleyside, Cragside is an extraordinary Victorian country home near Rothbury, Northumberland. Built in 1880, it was the most technologically advanced house of its time – the first in the world to be lit using hydroelectric power, with a water-powered laundry, dishwasher, dumb waiter, hydraulic passenger lift, hydroelectric rotisserie and Turkish bath suite. What started as a modest country retreat ended up as a wonder of the Victorian age.

Cragside was the brainchild of the industrial genius William Armstrong (later Lord Armstrong), highly accomplished as an engineer, inventor, arms manufacturer, industrialist, philanthropist, environmentalist and landscape designer. He and his wife commissioned the British architect Richard Norman Shaw to design a home near Rothbury where

Above: *Clinging to the sides of the valley, Cragside is a technical achievement and packed full of innovations.*

Right: *Lit from above by a series of skylights, the Gallery formerly housed the museum.*

Armstrong had spent his childhood, and over the course of 15 years the project became part-house, part-castle, with a fusion of Gothic, Tudor and Jacobean elements.

The entrance hall was illuminated by 10,000 lamps and the palatial interior rooms were resplendent, with guests including the King of Siam, Shah of Persia, Crown Prince of Afghanistan, Prime Minister of China and Britain's Prince of Wales. The Armstrongs filled their house with a treasure trove of artworks, ceramics, furniture, crafts and gadgets (including one of the first telephones), and constructed ambitious gardens with five lakes, rocky crags, waterfalls, streams, bridges, rhododendron drifts and enormous conifer trees.

Armstrong died at Cragside in 1900, and much of his art collection was sold to pay his heirs' immense inheritance tax bill. In 1977, the house and estate were acquired by the National Trust, and were opened to the public two years later. Visitors can admire

the Library, described as 'Shaw's greatest domestic achievement', the Dining Room, with stained-glass windows designed by William Morris and a portrait of Armstrong and his dogs, the Owl Suite, named after the carved birds in the woodwork, the star-like lighting in the Gallery, the spectacular Drawing Room, with its elaborate inglenook fireplace, the Kitchens, with their technological aids, and the Turkish Bath, which doubled as the house's heating system.

Cragside was used as a film location in *The Current War* (2017) and *Jurassic World: Fallen Kingdom* (2018).

CHAPTER

7

ENGLAND
North West

Just two grand houses in the north west are covered here – but they are both superb examples of their type. Lyme Park has everything – a grand and beautiful house primarily in the Palladian style in the Cheshire Peak District, and since 1995, it has held a deep attachment for fans of Jane Austen's *Pride and Prejudice*. Arley Hall, with its medieval roots was remodelled in the 19th century to create a house in a hybrid style known as Jacobethan – with elements of both Elizabethan and Jacobean houses. It has lovely formal gardens and a richly decorated interior.

Lyme Park in Cheshire, one of the largest, yet most romantic of English houses.

Lyme Park

A 1,400-acre estate south of Disley in the Peak District, Lyme Park is Cheshire's largest house dating from the 1500s, with modifications made in the 1720s. It houses the Lyme Caxton Missal, containing the liturgy of the mass, published in 1487 by William Caxton, and it was the filming location of Pemberley in the 1995 adaptation of Jane Austen's *Pride and Prejudice*. The mansion is surrounded by 19th-century formal gardens and a medieval deer park, with far-reaching views across Manchester and the Cheshire Plain.

Sir Thomas Danyers owned the estate from 1346, and it passed to his daughter Margaret, who married Piers Legh in 1388. A dynasty of Leghs remained at Lyme Park until 1946 when it was given to the National Trust.

The first house, built in the mid-16th century, was demolished to make way for a new L-shaped

house. In 1725, the Italian architect Giacomo Leoni created a palatial Palladian residence. He left the Elizabethan Long Gallery, adding a new Bright Gallery running around three sides of a courtyard.

In 1898, many of Leoni's Palladian features were removed, the wall colours painted over, the chimney pieces removed, and the house returned to its Elizabethan roots. Once transferred to the National Trust, however, the Palladian décor was restored, and now Lyme Park mixes Tudor, Georgian and Victorian styles.

Visitors can view a mixture of Elizabethan plasterwork and panelling, 16th-century stained-glass, 17th-century tapestries, English clocks and carvings by Grinling Gibbons, and a lavish Baroque ceiling above the staircase. The formal gardens, Reflection Lake, Orangery and Rose Garden were created in the 19th and early 20th centuries. Lyme Park has also appeared in *Brideshead Revisited* (1981), *Far from the Madding Crowd* (1998), *The Forsyte Saga* (2002) and *The Awakening* (2011).

Lyme Park's romantic golden stone facade is set amidst rolling grounds in the Cheshire Peak District.

Arley Hall

Part of an estate that has belonged to the Warburton family since the 12th century, Arly Hall has elaborate ceilings and oak panelling, magnificent fireplaces and stained-glass windows, and the grounds include one of Britain's first and finest herbaceous borders, as well as a Gothic Revival chapel. The estate currently belongs to Michael Llowarch Warburton Flower, 11th Viscount Ashbrook.

Around 1758, the timber-framed medieval house was encased in brick and finished with stucco, and the landscape turned into a garden and park. In 1826, owner Rowland Egerton-Warburton commissioned local architect George Latham to redesign the Jacobean house in the Elizabethan style, resulting in a hybrid known as 'Jacobethan'. He also asked architect Anthony Salvin to build a chapel, and when Salvin presented him with a

selection of different Gothic styles, Rowland chose to have them all at once.

The front Entrance Hall is Jacobean, with rich panelling and an elaborate ceiling; the Grand Staircase is Latham's Elizabethan masterpiece, with oak stairs and doorways and panelled plasterwork; the Library is Victorian Gothic, with bookcases flooded with light from stained-glass windows; the plastered Drawing Room is beautifully gilded; the Emperor's Room – where Napoleon III lived in 1847–8 – is decorated with paintings by

Above: *A sunken garden and plentiful formal topiary in the formal gardens*

Left: *The distinctive 'Jacobethan' frontage of Arley Hall.*

Piers Egerton-Warburton. The 12-acre gardens, created in the 1850s, include a Tea Cottage, open lawns, herbaceous borders, fruit trees, kitchen garden, ha-ha and Clock Tower. A 1900 Flag Garden has floribunda roses and lavender.

The estate has been used as a location for several productions, including *The Adventures of Sherlock Holmes* (1984–5), *Evermoor* (2014) and *Peaky Blinders* (2016).

CHAPTER 8

WALES

Often thought of as the land of castles – and there are many complete examples built as fortresses in medieval times – Wales also has a rich history of stately homes. Tredegar House, home to the Morgan family, is a red-brick mansion dating from the 17th century and with many elaborate rooms to explore. Picton Castle was a medieval castle but was adapted and rebuilt to create a stately home using a mixture of new Georgian styling and its 13th-century towers. Powis Castle gained a grand terraced garden during its 17th-century remodelling, and holds a fascinating collection of artefacts through Edward Clive, who worked for the East India Company. Erdigg near Wrexham, is renowned for its fine interiors and 'upstairs, downstairs' portraits of owners and servants. And Plas Newydd on the Isle of Anglesey has one of the greatest viewpoints of any house.

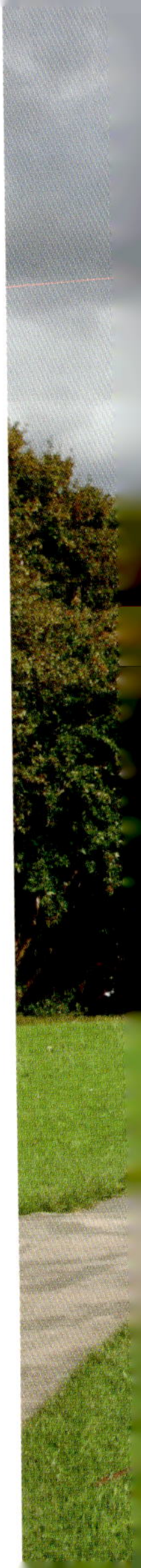

Plas Newydd on the coast in Anglesea was built in the 18th century in a mix of Gothic and classical styles.

Tredegar House

One of the most outstanding 17th-century stately homes in Britain, Tredegar House is a red-brick mansion in Newport, Wales. It belonged to the immensely wealthy Morgan family (later Lords Tredegar) for over 500 years, and stands within 90 acres of beautiful gardens and parkland.

The Morgans came to south Wales in the early 15th century and built a stone house (some of which survives today) on the site of a previously existing medieval house. The name comes from the Welsh *Tredegar Fawr*, the original farmstead. Over the years, the Morgan family amassed a fortune and acquired land, and from the 18th century they used their wealth to invest in the new industries of coal, iron, canals and railways. They welcomed high-status visitors – including Charles I – to Tredegar House, and then rebuilt and expanded it.

In 1854, British Army officer Godfrey Morgan, 1st Viscount Tredegar, took part in the Charge of the Light Brigade against

Left: *The grand main hall at Tredegar House.*

Right: *The house was rebuilt using red brick, a rare and expensive commodity in Wales.*

Russia in the Crimean War, and lived to tell the tale. A painting of his horse hangs in the house: the brave steed itself was buried in the grounds with full military honours.

The eccentric Evan Morgan, 2nd Viscount Tredegar, was the final Morgan at Tredegar House from 1929. He kept exotic birds and animals and threw extravagant parties, inviting guests such as H.G. Wells and high-profile Nazis, and ran through most of the family money. The house was taken over the by the National Trust in 2011.

Highlights include the 17th-century Gilt Room where the Morgans entertained and danced, the Brown Room's oak carvings of serpents, lions and griffins, the New Hall's portraits of kings and queens, the Victorian-style New Parlour with magnificent dining furniture, and the below-stairs Great Kitchen, still room, housekeeper's room and servants' hall. The 1930s King's Room has Evan's boxing kangaroo on display. Outside, the 18th-century estate includes three formal gardens – an Orchard Garden, Cedar Garden and Orangery Garden – set within extensive parklands, oak avenues and a lake.

Picton Castle

A medieval castle converted into an opulent home for the Philipps family in the 18th century, Picton Castle lies near Haverfordwest in Pembrokeshire, Wales. It features a unique combination of styles, with 13th-century towers and a gatehouse and Georgian interiors, making it the only building of its type in mainland Britain. It was occupied by the Philipps family until 1987, then given to a charitable trust.

The 13th-century castle was built by the judge Sir John de Wogan, Lord of Picton, on the site of an even older castle. Unusually, the new structure had no inner courtyard or keep, but seven circular towers, two of

which linked together to form a gatehouse – similar to several Irish castles built around the same time.

The estate passed to Sir Thomas Philipps in 1491, and by 1611 the family was wealthy and influential, inaugurating a line of baronets with Picton Castle as their family seat. Sir John Philipps, 4th Baronet, began making alterations to the structure in 1697. He enlarged the Great Hall to two storeys, making it an impressive focal point of the house.

Sir John Philipps, 6th Baronet, transformed the castle further in 1749–52, creating the elegant interiors that remain today, with plasterwork ceilings, wood panelling, sash windows and marbled fireplaces. A Georgian wing was added in the 1790s, completing the design.

Picton Castle is surrounded by a beautiful 40-acre garden, including a walled garden, pond, fernery, bluebell walk, herb garden and woodland.

Picton's castellated circular towers reflect the house's origins as a medieval castle.

Powis Castle

Originally a medieval stronghold, Powis Castle is a grand country mansion near Welshpool in Powys, Wales. It was transformed from a castle into a comfortable home by the Herbert family, and became the seat of the Earl of Powis. A tall structure with turrets and castellation, it is famous for its unique collection of Indian treasures belonging to the Clive family, as well as its world-renowned formal garden, Italianate terraces, parkland and deer park.

In 1578, the *c.*1200 castle was leased to Sir Edward Herbert, second son of the Earl of Pembroke and Anne Parr (Henry VIII's sister-in-law). In the 1680s, William Herbert, 1st Marquess of Powis, hired the architect William Winde to design outdoor terraces, grass slopes and an orangery. Several generations of Herberts altered the structure, adding a grand staircase with a ceiling painted by Antonio Verrio, walls painted by Verrio's pupil Gerard Lanscroon, an elaborately plastered and wood-panelled Elizabethan long gallery and a sumptuous ballroom.

In 1784, Henrietta Herbert married Edward Clive, the son of Robert Clive (Clive of India). After working for the East India Company and living in India for three years, Edward returned to Wales with a valuable collection of artefacts. Over 300 ivories, statues, ornaments, weapons and armour are on display in the Clive Museum at Powis Castle, including a jewelled gold tiger finial from the throne of Tipu Sultan, ruler of the Kingdom of Mysore in southern India, and a rare Roman marble cat.

This lavish house contains one of the finest collections of sculptures, furniture, tapestries and paintings in Wales, including a magnificent portrait of Henrietta Herbert by Sir Joshua Reynolds.

Powis Castle overlooking the glorious terraced gardens designed by William Winde in the 17th century.

Erddig

Located on a dramatic escarpment just outside Wrexham in Wales, Erddig was built in 1684–7 for Joshua Edisbury, High Sheriff of Denbighshire, then belonged to the Yorke family for 240 years and was rescued from dereliction in the 1970s. It contains a large collection of servants' portraits, giving visitors a unique insight into the relationship between the upstairs family and their below-stairs staff.

English lawyer and politician John Meller bought Erddig in 1714 and refurbished and expanded it, filling it with fine furnishings, fabrics and wallpapers.

When he died in 1733, the house passed to Meller's nephew Simon Yorke, and it remained with the Yorkes from then on.

In 1799, Simon's son Philip began keeping records of everyone who lived and worked on the estate, including portraits, photographs and verse. Philip also created a Saloon, Library and new Kitchen, and covered the west front of the house in stone.

Subsequent Yorkes built a magnificent Dining Room, installed underfloor heating and a bell system, and created a Music Room in the entrance hall. The 1,200-acre landscape pleasure park was designed by William Emes in 1768–80, who used a style similar to Lancelot 'Capability' Brown: naturalistic trees and water.

In 1973, Erddig was given to the National Trust, and it was restored and opened to the public in 1977. Visitors can admire John Meller's elegant rooms containing crimson wool and silk-covered chairs, silver-leaf seats in the Withdrawing Room, Chinese embroidered silk hangings and Soho tapestries in the Best Bedchamber, and blue damask in the Best Dressing Room. The 18th-century gardens feature a walled garden with rare fruit trees and pleached lime trees, long herbaceous borders, formal yew hedges, a national collection of ivies, a reflective pool and William Emes' circular 'Cup and Saucer' water feature.

Above: *The Dining Room at Erddig with its marble columns and finely detailed ceiling and cornicing.*

Left: *Erddig's elegant frontage, adorned in autumnal vines.*

Plas Newydd

Sitting majestically on the banks of the Menai Strait in Llanddaniel Fab near Anglesey, Wales, Plas Newydd – meaning 'new house' – is the ancestral home of the Marquess of Anglesey. It is an elegant 18th-century stately home in a mixture of classical and Gothic styles, and includes Italianate gardens and parklands with glorious views of the mountains of Snowdonia. The interior is famous for its enormous fantasy mural painted by Rex Whistler in 1936–8.

The 14th-century estate was owned by the Griffith family of Bangor, with the Great Hall being built in the 16th century and surviving to this day. By the 18th century, Plas Newydd passed to the Bayly family, who changed their name to Paget. Henry Paget fought at the Battle of Waterloo in 1815, losing a leg in the process, and his bravery and leadership garnered him the title of 1st Marquess of Anglesey. His wooden leg is on display in the house in the Waterloo exhibition.

The architect James Wyatt made changes to Plas Newydd in the late 18th century. Despite his nickname 'Wyatt the Destroyer', he retained the towers and hall, and merged neoclassical and Gothic styles together, creating a fashionable new mansion. In 1799, the famous landscape gardener Humphry Repton designed the gardens with naturalistic drifts of trees and shrubs.

The 5th Marquess converted the chapel to a theatre in the late 19th century, and his son, the 6th Marquess, combined three servants' rooms to make a large Dining Room. This room became famous when Marjorie Paget, 6th Marchioness of Anglesey, commissioned Rex Whistler to paint a huge Italianate mural – his

largest work. Measuring more than 58 feet in length, the *trompe l'oeil* masterpiece depicts British and Italian churches and castles in an imagined Mediterranean seaport, with boats and ships in the harbour and the mountains of Snowdonia in the background, and is a highlight of any visit to Plas Newydd.

Plas Newydd has an enviable vantage point overlooking the Menai Straits across to mainland Wales and Snowdonia.

The estate was taken over by the National Trust and opened to the public in 1976.

CHAPTER 9

SCOTLAND

With a treasure trove of great houses, Scotland is a delight for the lover of stately homes. Floors Castle in the Scottish Borders is a wonderfully detailed 18th-century palace, while not too far away, Abbotsford House is imbued with the spirit of its most famous owner, the novelist Sir Walter Scott. Dumfries House in Ayrshire was saved as a complete house and contents through the intervention of the Prince of Wales. Mount Stuart House on Bute is an elaborate 19th-century house in the Gothic Revival style. The Palace of Holyroodhouse was built next to the ruined abbey and is official home for the British monarch in Scotland. The classical Hopetoun House and Gosford House both lie on the shores of the Firth of Forth. Falkland Palace is an example of Scottish Renaissance architecture while Dunrobin Castle is a 19th-century palace in the Scottish Baronial style.

The gorgeous confection that is Dunrobin Castle set atop its beautiful gardens.

Floors Castle

Floors Castle (pronounced 'Floor-ers') is the seat of the Duke of Roxburghe. The building was designed by William Adam, and the name is believed to come from the French *fleurs* meaning 'flowers'. The house is well known for its appearance in the film *Greystoke: The Legend of Tarzan, Lord of the Apes* (1984).

In 1721, John Ker, 1st Duke of Roxburghe, wanted a home to reflect his status, so he commissioned William Adam to create a Georgian neoclassical building incorporating a former stone tower house on the site. Adam included a walled garden, formal parterre and woodland walks, all of which remain today.

When James Innes-Ker, 6th Duke of Roxburghe, married in 1836, he hired one of the greatest Scottish architects of the day, William Playfair, to transform the house. The result was a masterpiece, with Renaissance-style

spires, domes, cupolas, turrets and battlements, giving the house the appearance of a fairy-tale castle.

The interior rooms were flamboyantly redecorated in the 1920s by the 8th Duke's wife, the wealthy American heiress Mary Goelet, who collected 17th-century Gobelin tapestries, furniture from the Palace of Versailles and paintings by Thomas Gainsborough, Henry Raeburn, Henri Matisse and Pablo Picasso.

The gardens include a 4-acre walled garden with Victorian glasshouses, fruit trees, an oak-framed fruit cage and stunning flower borders. The formal Millennium Garden features the massive intertwined initials of the 10th Duke and Duchess ('G' for Guy, 'V' for Virginia and 'R' for Roxburghe), together with the Queen's House that was built especially for Queen Victoria to take her afternoon tea.

Right: *The living room at Floors Castle, featuring some of its French tapestries.*

Below: *The amazingly complex exterior of Floors Castle with its plethora of finely designed roof details.*

Abbotsford House

The home of the 19th-century novelist and poet Sir Walter Scott (author of such works as *The Lady of the Lake*, *Rob Roy* and *Ivanhoe*), Abbotsford is located on the banks of the River Tweed in the Scottish Borders. Scott designed the house himself, so it embodies his own tastes, talents and interests, as well as the wider Romantic style of the day.

Cartleyhole, a modest farmhouse originally stood on the site and was bought by Scott in 1811. He renamed it Abbotsford after the Tweed River ford used by the abbots of Melrose Abbey. Architect William Atkinson expanded it to create a grand mansion. The Scottish interior designer David Ramsay Hay decorated the ornate interiors.

Left: *In the library are many books about witchcraft, with eyewitness accounts of the Salem witch trials.*

Opposite: *The modest house was remade to fit Scott's romantic ideals.*

Scott was an avid collector of books, artefacts, furniture, weaponry and various curiosities, and the house reflected his enthusiasms. The architectural style is Scottish Baronial – like a castle in miniature, with towers and battlements along the walls. The large rectangular building features an impressive Entrance Hall and Drawing Room, but the Library and Study are the real stars. The floor-to-ceiling shelves are filled with dictionaries, horticultural reference books, lecture notes from Scott's days as a law student, poems written to his first love, the first book of fairy tales by the Brothers Grimm, nearly 5,000 chapbooks (humorous volumes containing popular ballads and risqué poetry) and a 15th-century 'lost' illuminated manuscript telling the legends of English and Welsh saints. Queen Victoria visited Abbotsford House on her first trip to Scotland, and loved it so much that she remodelled Balmoral Castle in the same style.

Outdoors, there are three distinct garden areas: a walled garden, formal entrance courts and a woodland. Notable features include a Rapunzel tower, a greenhouse based on a medieval jousting tent and a heritage vegetable garden.

Dumfries House

A Palladian country home in Ayrshire in Scotland, Dumfries House was built as a kind of 'honey trap' for the widowed 5th Earl of Dumfries to attract a new wife. It is famous for its world-class collection of 18th-century furniture, especially pieces made by Thomas Chippendale.

Originally the site of Lefnoreis Castle, the estate was inherited in 1742 by William Dalrymple-Crichton, 5th Earl of Dumfries, who transformed the house. Building began in 1754 and William's wife died two years later. He mourned her deeply, but decided to create an elegant home for a new wife – to provide him with an heir.

Dumfries House was completed in 1759, and William decorated it with colourful and stylish interiors. He also filled it with the most fashionable furniture of the day,

Left and right: *The 5th Earl commissioned the Scottish architect brothers John and Robert Adam to replace the stone castle with a finely proportioned house featuring a three-storey central block and wings linking smaller pavilions.*

including many examples from the workshop of Thomas Chippendale.

William did marry a second time, but the marriage did not provide an heir so the house passed to his nephew Patrick McDouall-Crichton, 6th Earl of Dumfries. From there it went to Patrick's daughter Lady Elizabeth McDouall-Crichton, who married John, Lord Mount Stuart, in 1792, intertwining two of Scotland's most prominent families. Their son John Crichton-Stuart became the 2nd Marquess of Bute.

Dumfries House remained in the Crichton-Stuart family until 2007, when it was sold to the nation. Highlights include the Chippendale writing desk in the Study, the Pink Dining Room with ornate Rococo ceiling, the gilded Family Parlour with vibrant yellow silk damask furniture, the Family Bedroom's four-poster Chippendale bed, the Blue Drawing Room's Chippendale chairs and bookcase and first-ever Axminster carpet, the Pewter Corridor's domed painted ceiling, and the Tapestry Room's Greco-Roman tapestries.

A restoration project included the creation of the 5-acre Queen Elizabeth walled garden – one of the largest in Scotland. Visitors can also explore the Rothesay Garden, Woodland Garden, Education Garden and Front Garden.

Mount Stuart House

Situated on the Isle of Bute in Scotland, Mount Stuart House is a 19th-century Gothic Revival mansion created for the 3rd Marquess of Bute (who formerly owned Dumfries House) with richly decorated interiors and expansive gardens. It has a heated indoor swimming pool, and was the first house in Scotland to be illuminated by electricity.

The original house was built in 1719 but destroyed by fire in 1887. John Crichton-Stuart, 3rd Marquess of Bute, replaced it with a grander house to reflect his high status, religious ideals, and special interest in astrology. He commissioned Sir Robert Rowland Anderson to design a flamboyant palace rather than a house and it took 21 years to build.

Two of the original wings survived the fire, and these were incorporated into the new building, their white colour standing out starkly from the new

red sandstone. The exterior is filled with decorative arches and windows, intricate stone carvings and an eaves gallery running around the top.

The interiors are awe-inspiring and were designed to impress. The Marble Chapel, made from white Carrara marble, has geometric Cosmati flooring in the same style as the Sistine Chapel and Westminster Abbey. The Dining Room contains 18th-century portraits by Allan Ramsay, Joshua Reynolds and Thomas Gainsborough, and is decorated with foraging squirrels carved into the wood panelling.

The 300-acre gardens reflect the Bute family's passion for horticulture. The Wee Garden, Kitchen Garden and Rock Garden are a source of globally significant flowers and produce, and a Pinetum features imposing conifers dating back to the Victorian era.

Below: *The architectural style is a combination of Venetian and Gothic.*

Right: *The Marble Hall has a domed ceiling 80 ft high surrounded by stained-glass windows depicting the signs of the zodiac.*

Palace of Holyroodhouse

Also known as Holyrood Palace, the Palace of Holyroodhouse is located in Edinburgh at the end of the Royal Mile, and is the official residence of the British monarch in Scotland. Scottish royals have lived there since the 16th century, and it is historically best known as the home of Mary, Queen of Scots. Today, Queen Elizabeth II spends a week in the State Apartments at the beginning of every summer while carrying out official engagements in Scotland.

The site dates back to an Augustinian monastery founded by David I of Scotland in 1128,

Below: *The imposing entrance to the Palace with its characteristic roof turrets.*

Right: *The Royal Dining Room at Holyroodhouse, fit for a monarch in residence.*

and the name refers to a relic of Christ's cross, known as the 'Holy Rood'. In 1501, the abbey was replaced with a Gothic house for James IV and his new queen Margaret Tudor (Henry VIII's sister), and included a Great Hall, Gallery, Royal Apartments and a Chapel. James V renovated the house in 1528, transforming it into a grand palace with an enormous north tower and new west façade.

In 1542, James V was succeeded by his daughter Mary when she was only six days old, and she lived at the Palace of Holyroodhouse as Mary, Queen of Scots from 1561 to 1567. Her Bedchamber is described as 'the most famous room in Scotland': her private secretary David Rizzio was stabbed to death just outside it by a group led by her jealous second husband, Lord Darnley, in 1566, all within earshot of Mary dining downstairs. The Bedchamber has been preserved exactly as it was then, with magnificent paintings and tapestries, a sumptuous four-poster bed and an oak-panelled ceiling bearing Mary's parents' initials. The Outer Chamber still has the alleged blood stain where Rizzio's body fell.

In the 1670s, Charles II commissioned the Scottish architect Sir William Bruce to remodel much of the house, blending old with new. A second tower was added to provide symmetry to James V's tower, and a first-floor suite of ornate Royal Apartments was built around a classical central quadrangle.

During the Jacobite Rising of 1745, Charles Edward Stuart ('Bonnie Prince Charlie') briefly held court at Holyroodhouse while attempting to take the throne, after which the palace was neglected for some years. The roof of the abbey collapsed in 1768, and has remained open to the elements ever since.

Above: *A semi-aerial view of the Palace, showing how it sits within the grounds*

Right: *The ruins of Holyrood Abbey, which adjoins Holyroodhouse.*

In 1822, George IV visited Scotland and held a reception at Holyrood. Seeing the dilapidated state of the interiors, he asked for repairs to be made but to keep Mary's rooms preserved. More renovations were carried out for Queen Victoria in 1850, with Renaissance-style exterior work by Robert Matheson and interiors by the decorator David Ramsay Hay.

George V and Queen Mary continued to restore and modernize the palace from 1910. They put in new bathrooms, a lift and central heating, and held summer garden parties in the grounds – a tradition that remains to this day. A Throne Room containing two Morris & Co. thrones was also added.

Visitors can see the 16th-century apartments of Mary, Queen of Scots, the sumptuously decorated State Apartments with their plasterwork ceilings, wood panelling, paintings and tapestries, and the Great Gallery lined with portraits of all the Scottish monarchs, where Elizabeth II carries out investitures and holds state banquets. Outside, the romantic ruins of Holyrood Abbey remain as they were in the 12th century, and the royal gardens inspired by Prince Albert's original designs have been restored.

A ghost is said to wander the palace and grounds at night – she is a Scottish healer named Agnes Sampson, who was executed at Holyrood for witchcraft in 1592.

Hopetoun House

Located on the shores of the Firth of Forth near South Queensferry, Hopetoun House is often described as Scotland's finest stately home. It is a supreme example of 18th-century architecture, the older part designed by Sir William Bruce with later additions by William Adam. The panoramic view of the façade is awe-inspiring, with a long, straight driveway bisecting two enormous lawns at the front and a reflective Round Pond at the back. The 6,500-acre grounds include a Spring Garden Trail, bowling green, woodland walks, deer park and Sea Walk Trail.

The estate has belonged to the Hope family since the late 1600s, with Sir John Hope and his wife Lady Margaret deciding to build a grand stately home on the site. John lost his life at sea in 1682 but Margaret saw the plans through, commissioning Sir William Bruce to design a home for her soon-to-be-married son Charles. The

construction of a central building flanked by two projecting wings took place from 1699 to 1707.

Charles became 1st Earl of Hopetoun during this period, and in 1721 he decided to turn the already grand mansion into something even more majestic. He commissioned the foremost Scottish architect of the day, William Adam, to enlarge and remodel the house, and the interiors were completed by Adam's two famous sons, John and Robert.

The front of the house that we see today is William Adam's ornate Baroque work, while the back is in the more classical style of William Bruce. The 'Bruce House' includes the 1st Earl's Bedchamber, oak-panelled Garden Room and octagonal Main Staircase decorated with intricate woodcarvings. The 'Adam House' includes the huge Entrance Hall, Drawing Rooms and State Dining Room, all embellished with opulent Georgian carvings, gilding, plasterwork, furniture, paintings, tapestries and clocks.

Hopetoun House is open to the public but remains the home of the present Lord Hopetoun. It is the setting for the television series *Outlander* (2014–).

The front of the main house showcases the style of William Adam, the master of ornate Baroque architecture.

Gosford House

The seat of the Charteris family (the Earls of Wemyss and March), Gosford House is located on the south side of the Firth of Forth in East Lothian, Scotland. The outstanding neoclassical mansion sits within 5,000 acres of parkland and coastline, and was the product of two designs: it started as one of the final commissions of the revered Scottish architect Robert Adam, and was completed in 1800 by William Young.

The estate was purchased in 1781 by the Scottish landowner Francis Wemyss-Charteris (later 7th Earl of Wemyss), and in 1790 he asked Robert Adam to build a new house next to the existing building, in which to display his collection of paintings.

Adam died in 1792 before the house was completed, and his plans were taken over and altered by William Young. The two wings designed by Adam were demolished by the 8th Earl of Wemyss, but rebuilt in 1891 by the 10th Earl, following Young's designs. The three-storey Marble Hall is the house's most impressive feature, with an enormous double staircase and picture gallery

Both architects who worked on Gosford House left their mark: Adam in the windows and Young in the plasterwork and colonnades.

above – the 10th Earl collected many paintings by Italian and Dutch masters. The styles of the two architects remain: Adam's Palladian windows, and Young's ornate plasterwork and colonnades.

The Walled Kitchen Garden, Gardener's Cottage and Bothy were built in 1853. The parklands include a pyramidal Mausoleum (where the 7th Earl is buried), Lily Pond, Ice House, Curling House and Boat and Bath House, with surrounding plantations of woodland.

The house was occupied by the army in World War II. Although it sustained some serious fire damage in 1940, most of the contents were saved and restored.

Films shot there include *The House of Mirth* (2000) and *The Awakening* (2011).

Falkland Palace

The country retreat of the Stuart kings and queens of Scotland, Falkland Palace is a magnificent Renaissance estate in Falkland, Fife. It is also home to the world's oldest real (royal) tennis court, dating back to 1539.

There was a hunting lodge on the site in the 12th century, and this was expanded into a castle for the Earls of Fife in the 13th century. From 1501 to 1541, James IV and his son James V transformed the castle into a 'pleasure palace', as the need to impress their peers outweighed the need for a defensive structure. A Great Hall for state occasions was built in James IV's time, then James V commissioned the best masons in Europe to copy the style of the grand châteaux of France, adding a great twin-towered Gatehouse at the entrance

Left: *Falkland Palace, a Scottish Renaissance gem.*
Right: *The Chapel Room at the Palace, rebuilt during substantial renovations from 1887.*

and a four-walled tennis court for royalty to enjoy the 'sport of kings'. The finished palace is now one of Scotland's finest examples of Renaissance architecture.

It soon became a favourite retreat for many royal residents, including Mary, Queen of Scots, who enjoyed horse-riding, tennis, falconry and hunting for stag and wild boar.

The palace suffered years of neglect after a fire in 1654, until a comprehensive restoration project was put into action in 1887 by John Crichton-Stuart, 3rd Marquess of Bute. The Chapel Royal was rebuilt and is now renown as one of the finest pre-Reformation chapels in Scotland. The wood panelling and painted ceilings of the Royal Apartments were restored, and visitors can see James VI's canopied bed in the King's Bedchamber, tapestries and replicas of 16th- and 17th-century furniture in the Gatehouse and the exquisitely painted walls of the Library.

The extensive formal gardens were designed by Percy Cane in 1946, and the grounds include an orchard, willow labyrinth, fishpond, wildflower meadow and physic garden with Renaissance herbal remedies. The Falkland Palace Royal Tennis Club has been running since 1975.

Dunrobin Castle

Looking every bit the fairy-tale palace with slender white spires and French-style formal gardens, Dunrobin Castle is a stately home in Sutherland in the Scottish Highlands, overlooking the Dornoch Firth. It is the family seat of the Earl or Countess of Sutherland and the Clan Sutherland, and the most northerly of Britain's stately homes. Dating back to the early 1300s, it is also one of Britain's oldest continually inhabited houses.

The original fortification was founded by Earl Robin in 1275, the name coming from the Gaelic *Dun Robin*, meaning 'Robin's Fort'. Some of the structure dating back to the 1320s has been preserved in the interior courtyard, and the Earls of Sutherland made various additions during the 17th and 18th centuries.

In the 19th century, George Sutherland-Leveson-Gower, 2nd Duke of Sutherland, decided to have the castle remodelled for his large family. He commissioned Sir Charles Barry (who had worked on the Palace of Westminster, Highclere Castle and Harewood House) to design a home in the Scottish Baronial style, with formal gardens modelled on those at the Palace of Versailles in Paris. Work took place between 1835 and 1850, and the completed house was described by Queen Victoria as 'a mixture of an old Scottish castle and a French château'.

Dunrobin Castle was used as a naval hospital during World War I, then the Scottish architect Sir Robert Lorimer made renovations after the war. Following a period as a boys' boarding school (1965–72), the house was opened to the public in 1973.

Visitors can explore some of the finest interiors in Scotland, all filled with antique furniture, paintings, china and silver. Highlights include the Dining Room with wood-panelled walls and table set with the family silver, the intricately decorated Drawing Room with Louis XVI furniture, the Green and Gold Bedroom with a four-poster bed made especially for Queen Victoria, and the Library with over 10,000 books and a portrait of Duchess Eileen, wife of the 5th Duke of Sutherland.

The gardens include three circular parterres with a pool and fountain in the middle of each one, an area for falconry displays and a croquet lawn, with panoramic views southwards across the Moray Firth towards the Cairngorms.

Dunrobin is a true storybook palace with its myriad round towers and sharply pointed spires.

10

CHAPTER

NORTHERN IRELAND

Some of the most elegant houses in the UK are to be found in Northern Ireland. Just a few are shown here but they are all worth visiting. Hillsborough Castle in County Down is the official residence of the monarch in Northern Ireland and dates from the late 18th century. Mount Stewart House is another Georgian mansion that underwent a number of changes during the 19th century and has a garden that has been voted one of the world's greatest. Florence Court in County Fermanagh lies on a grand estate and has graceful Georgian interiors.

Stunning spring gardens at Mount Stewart House in County Down.

Hillsborough Castle

Located in the village of Hillsborough in County Down, Hillsborough Castle is the official residence of the Queen and other members of the royal family when visiting Northern Ireland, and also home of the Secretary of State for Northern Ireland. The 18th-century Georgian country house was owned by the Hill family until 1922, then sold to the British government.

Wills Hill, 1st Marquess of Downshire and Earl of Hillsborough, held the position of Secretary of State for the Colonies from 1768 until 1772, just before the American War of Independence. As befitting a diplomat of his status, he built a country home – known in Ireland as a 'big house' – near a fort already on the site. One of American's founding fathers, Benjamin Franklin, was among his first guests in 1771.

The mansion was built as a townhouse on one side of a Georgian square, and parties and celebrations held there were extraordinarily grand. An astonishing 3,500 guests sat down to dinner at the 4th Marquess of Downshire's wedding in 1837 and the event was reported in the Ulster Times as 'a fête... almost without parallel in the kingdom'.

The steps to the front entrance of Hillsborough Castle. Queen Elizabeth II and Prince Philip stayed at Hillsborough during a 2002 tour of Northern Ireland.

The elegant State Rooms include the majestic Throne Room, State Dining Room and State Drawing Room, the last of which was the location for the signing of the Anglo-Irish Agreement by Margaret Thatcher and Garret FitzGerald in 1985.

Mo Mowlam, Tony Blair's Northern Ireland Secretary in the late 1990s, was very fond of Lady Grey's Study (named after the wife of the last Governor of Northern Ireland), and conducted meetings there while negotiating the Good Friday Peace Agreement of 1998. Prime Minister Tony Blair met US President George W. Bush in the same room in 2003 to discuss the progress of the Iraq War.

The gardens date from the 1760s, and include a Walled Garden, Granville Garden, Moss Walk, Yew Tree Walk, Willow House, Lost Garden, Summer House, Glen, Hydro House, Pinetum, Ice House and Lake, as well as the delightful Lady Alice's Temple, named after the daughter of the 4th Marquess of Downshire.

Mount Stewart

Situated on the shores of Strangford Lough in County Down, Mount Stewart is the Irish seat of the Marquess of Londonderry. The estate dates back to 1744 when it was owned by the Stewart family (later the Vane-Tempest-Stewarts). The grand house reflects the family's rich history, and the exquisite gardens are ranked among the top ten in the world.

Originally known as Mount Pleasant, the 18th-century house underwent changes with each successive Marquess of Londonderry. The London architect George Dance designed a west wing in 1804–6, and the Irish architect William Morrison added a large portico to the 11-bay entrance in 1835. Meanwhile, the house's collection of paintings, furniture and treasures grew. The 4th,

5th and 6th Marquesses, however, lived elsewhere, and the house suffered years of neglect.

After World War I, Charles Vane-Tempest-Stewart, 7th Marquess of Londonderry, and his wife Lady Edith breathed new life into Mount Stewart. Edith grew up at Dunrobin Castle in Scotland, and decided to transform Mount Stewart into a similarly grand home. She redecorated the interiors and filled the rooms with colour and scent, and replaced the relatively plain grounds with magnificent formal gardens.

The octagonal Central Hall has the feel of a cathedral, with a white Scrabo stone floor laid out in a radiating pattern. The Staircase is dominated by a painting of a famous racehorse – one of the most significant masterpieces in Ireland, *Hambletonian, Rubbing Down* by George Stubbs (1799–1800). The Dining Room has Empire chairs from the Congress of Vienna, each with an embroidered coat of arms. The Chapel has an intricately painted ceiling and stained-glass windows, and is festooned with Londonderry Knights of the Garter banners and Italian paintings.

The 950-acre gardens showcase Lady Edith's exceptional degree of artistry. There are a series of distinctive formal gardens – Sunk, Shamrock, Italian, Spanish and Mairi – as well as orchards, lakes, follies, woodland and farmland.

Left: *Palms and other exotic plants in the gardens at Mount Stewart.*

Right: *The vivid entrance hall at Mount Stewart with its chequerboard floor and black marble columns.*

Florence Court

Set against a wild mountain backdrop near Enniskillen in County Fermanagh, Florence Court is a beautiful Georgian mansion that was home to the Cole family, the Earls of Enniskillen, until 1973. It features a magnificent golden-grey façade, fine Irish furniture and stunning Rococo plasterwork, and the gardens include one of the country's most important trees, an 18th-century yew that has provided cuttings for almost every churchyard in Ireland.

Above: *The entrance hall at Florence Court in 1894, with trophy antlers and an array of spears and other weapons.*

Right: *The elegance of Florence Court is in sharp contrast to its wild surroundings.*

The original house was built in c.1719 for Sir John Cole and his wife Florence, hence the name. Their son John, 1st Lord Mount Florence, replaced it with a larger Palladian-style house around 1750, and commissioned the Dublin plasterer Robert West to decorate the interiors with elaborate plasterwork.

William Cole, 1st Earl of Enniskillen, made further changes in 1771, adding colonnades and pavilions, and William King designed a landscaped park with a curved main avenue replacing the straight drive.

The rooms are rich in detail, with some of the best Rococo plasterwork in Ireland – the high ceilings are decorated with dramatic swirling scrolls, palmettes, flower motifs and swags. There are also family portraits, 18th-century Irish furniture and an Aubusson carpet.

An ornamental Pleasure Ground was created in the 1840s, providing panoramic views over Benaughlin and Cuilcagh mountains, and the gardens include a thatched Summer House, Walled Garden, Sawmill and Ice House.

In 1953, Florence Court was given to the National Trust by John Cole, 5th Earl of Enniskillen. A fire caused serious damage not long afterwards, but the Trust was able to restore the building and its ornate interior plasterwork by referring to photographs and records.

The house appears in the television series *Blandings* (2013) and *The Woman in White* (2018), and in the film *Miss Julie* (2014).

Picture Credits

Alamy: 29 Michael Dunlea, 170, Jim Monk, 217 The National Trust Photolibrary

Diomedia: 19 Victoria and Albert Museum London UK, 38 Heritage Images/Historic England, 43 Mary Evans, 64 DeAgostini/S. Vannini, 81 National Media Museum London UK, 99 Heritage Images, 113 Heritage Images/English Heritage, 127 Heritage Images/The Print Collector, 197 DeAgostini/S. Vannini, 221 WestEnd61 RM/Martin Siepmann.

Getty Images: 59 Matthew Lloyd

Shutterstock: 2, 4, 7, 8, 11, 15, 17, 18, 20, 22, 25, 26, 30, 33, 35, 36, 37, 39, 40, 42, 44, 45, 46, 47, 49, 50, 53, 54, 55, 56, 58, 61, 63, 68, 70, 72, 73, 75, 77, 78, 79, 80, 84, 85, 86, 91, 93, 97, 100, 107, 109, 110, 112, 114, 115, 116, 117, 118, 123, 126, 129, 131, 135, 136, 142, 145, 149, 152, 159, 160, 162, 164, 166, 172, 174, 177, 178, 180, 181, 183, 185, 186, 189, 193, 195, 196, 198, 200, 201, 204, 205, 206, 207, 208, 211, 212, 215, 218, 223

Wikimedia Commons: 23, 27, 31, 32, 34, 48, 65, 67, 74, 82, 87, 88, 89, 90, 92, 94, 95, 102, 103, 104, 108, 121, 122, 124, 125, 128, 133, 138, 139, 140, 141, 143, 144, 146, 147, 150, 151, 153, 154, 155, 156, 157, 168, 169, 175, 184, 190, 191, 199, 202, 203, 213, 220, 222